Let's Talk Life:

A NEW PERSPECTIVE

Words to Motivate, Inspire and Transform the Way You Think

By Nicole Ross

Let's Talk Life: A New Perspective
Words to Motivate, Inspire and Transform the Way You Think
by Nicole Ross

Printed in the United States of America
ISBN 9781628712797

www.xulonpress.com

DEDICATION

This book is dedicated to two women who laid the foundation for me a long time ago. To my grandmothers, Florence Thompson and Geraldine Faulkner. Thank you for the example that you have set. Thank you for your unconditional love and support. Thank you just for being you. I love you!

CONTENTS

INTRO

One of the problems troubling many people today is that while they feel overwhelmed with everything they have going on around them, there isn't much guidance to help them carry out their true purpose and destiny in life. Communication is the key to changing this. Successful dialogue is a must in order for people to really be able to find strength in one another, because you must understand that you are not in this alone.

Let's Talk Life is a book created to help people deal with the every-day hustle and bustle of life. People do not have much free time, so if you get an opportunity to read, I'm sure you want to make a deposit into your spirit. You want to read words of encouragement and inspiration that will uplift and help push you through whatever season in life you are currently in. Life as we know it is all about purpose and destiny. It is about finding your purpose and finding a way to live out that purpose. Life is full of good, bad and some in-between seasons. How you deal with each of these periods is the story of your life and what makes you who you are. As time passes by and you gain more and more experience, you still may never fully comprehend what life is all about.

Sometimes you see failure in life, but God sees victory in you. God sees in you what you cannot see in yourself. As we begin this book, I'd like to first share with you eight thought-transformational principles. While reading these principles, I'd like you to meditate upon them and really get them down in your spirit.

1) It does not matter if the enemy is aware of your assignment. If you are called of the Lord, God will not revoke His calling. It's up to you, however, to put the enemy in his place. You must purpose in your heart to do the things that God has called you to do and be what God has called you to be. It is a choice that you must make.

2) God is only obligated to His covenant (His Word), hence the importance of knowing the word of God for yourself. Let's just be real for

a moment: your Bible needs to be opened more than just on Sundays. God is not moved by your feelings, but by your faith in Him. Faith cometh by hearing, hearing by the word of God. He will be faithful to deliver you if you are faithful to believe Him and stand on His word.

3) Satan hates for you to gain a greater understanding of God's word because true revelation can change any situation and bring deliverance. Once again, know the word of God. Study it on a daily basis. Ask God for wisdom and understanding while reading and He will give it to you. If you don't understand a specific version, there are several other versions you should try. I am sure you can find one that will help you gain a better understanding while reading.

4) Do not allow the devil's beliefs to be greater than yours. Satan believes there is a God; he believes that Jesus is the son of God; he believes that hell exists, that his time is short and that Jesus will one day return. Satan believes, but he is lost. It's really unfortunate when satan has more belief in scripture than some Christians. Think on that for a moment, and make up in your mind

that no matter what, you will never let the enemy out-believe you.

5) Stop making satan appear bigger than he really is. Quit giving him credit for everything. Do not exaggerate his ability. Satan's kingdom does not have more power, but one thing it does have is lots of experience. His kingdom can initiate an attack, because that is what he does (he comes to steal, kill and destroy), but it cannot determine the outcome. He can plan an attack against you, but he cannot determine when or how the Lord is going to bring you out because yes, indeed, the Lord will bring you out.

6) Do not try to explain why a battle has come. Once you make the decision to live for God, you better believe that the enemy is not happy. You should anticipate nothing more than a fight and nothing less than a victory. Know what you are fighting against. Evil spirits work through people. Without the voice, hands and feet of a human being an evil spirit is limited in what it can achieve. This is why the Bible says in Ephesians 6:12 that we wrestle not against flesh and blood, but against principalities, against powers, against the rulers of the darkness of this world, against

spiritual wickedness in high places. When you know what you are fighting against, you will be prepared with the word of God and fight on your knees. While fighting, take heart in the fact that often the greatest battles precede the biggest blessings.

7) You must pray, fast and develop an intimate relationship with God in order to exercise true spiritual authority. Spiritual maturity must accompany spiritual authority. When you pray, do so with a spirit of expectation. Be very specific in your prayers and expect to hear from God. When you finish speaking, stay there and listen. Give God His time, just as you give everything else and everyone else theirs. You have to take authority over the enemy while spending time with God, whether it is in prayer or while reading the word. It is so important to put your flesh under submission because the enemy will easily try and distract you to prevent you from being able to truly hear the voice of God. Listen to your inner ear. When you have the Holy Ghost inside of you, you have an inner ear speaking to you, helping you and guiding you along your daily journey.

8) The word grace refers to the unmerited favor of God. The grace of God enables you to go places others cannot, do things others will not, and experience things others have not. Because of God's grace He allows seasons of refreshing in our lives. He will not allow battle after battle to continuously hit you without seeing miracles and answers to prayer. Your testimony is the words you have to say when you have passed the test and those miracles begin to happen. The Bible declares that we overcome by the blood of the Lamb and by the word of our testimony.

This thing called life can be a tough journey. It is imperative that we utilize all the tools and resources that God gives, because they really are the only things that will help lighten the load. Make it a point to operate in the power and authority placed on the inside of you on a daily basis. The more you apply these thought transformational principles to your life, the stronger you will be. Do not allow fear to have any place in your life. When you follow Jesus, He does not want you to have any fear. Perfect love casts out all fear and His love is perfect towards us. Lastly, be rooted and grounded in LOVE. Love is the basis of salvation and you should walk in love at all times, just as Jesus did. He is your perfect example.

I hope and pray these words of not only inspiration, but reality will help you bring together the pieces of a beautiful canvas picture that God has created of your life. There is so much that God has in store for His children. I truly believe that if you begin to stand on His word and apply it to the chaos surrounding your life, you will truly become the man or woman that God has called you to be. If you learn to be committed, loyal, develop a routine, spend time in prayer, gain strategy, focus and make up in your mind that you will be who God has called you to be your life can and will be changed forever. Now, Let's Talk Life!

GET YOUR MIND RIGHT

It's amazing how one's perception can affect so many things. Let's face it; life is just that... life. Stuff happens, a lot of which we have no control over. What you can control however is your perception and how you handle those things that do happen. Instead of looking at seemingly not so good situations as trouble, switch your perspective, find the positive and decide to approach it as an opportunity.

As a child of God, it is so important that you take the opportunity to show God how much you love and trust Him each and every day. In every aspect of your life. God is omniscience, which means He is all knowing. He already knows what is going to happen before it ever actually does. He just wants to see how you are going to process it. He wants to see if you believe His word and you really do trust Him with all things. I find it interesting how we can trust Him with our children or our jobs, but when it comes to other situations like our marriage or our finances we tend to want to handle those on our own. You cannot pick and choose; God wants to be God over every aspect of your life, not just what you want to Him to be in charge of.

You have to change your perspective. How do you change your perspective? Study the word of God. The more you study the Bible, the more you will know. As you learn more, that is where the transformation begins to take place. This will also help build your personal relationship with God. In addition to reading and learning more about the word, pray and ask God to help you. God never intended for you to change yourself. He wants to do it, after all, He is the one who created us, but you just have to ask.

There is nothing better than seeing first-hand the changes that God is doing within you. Not only seeing, but feeling the difference when something transpires that to the world wouldn't seem good at all, however you see it as an opportunity to trust God. Today's decisions are tomorrow's reality. Don't let short-term passions destroy long term blessings! Choose peace, choose love, choose joy, choose perseverance, choose faith, and most importantly choose a Godly perspective! It's time to get your mind right.

Life Tools:

Philippians 2:5 KJV "Let this mind be in you, which was also in Christ Jesus:"

Galatians 5:22-23 NKJV "But the fruit of the Spirit is love, joy, peace, longsuffering, kindness, goodness, faithfulness, gentleness, self-control. Against such there is no law."

HOW TO DEAL

How do you deal with people who do something or say something that you don't like? How do you deal with people who do something or say something that you do like? As a very outspoken person, my response is typically to verbally respond to that person and let them person know how I feel, especially when it is something I do not like. As I've grown and matured over time, I've learned that every situation needs to be dealt with appropriately. This can sometimes mean closing my mouth and not saying anything at all. The best thing you can do is actually use the situation as an opportunity to learn. Humble yourself and ask God to keep you. Ask Him to help prevent you from dealing with people in a way that is not pleasing to Him.

If folks do something that doesn't sit well with you, instead of getting upset or angry use it as an opportunity to learn what not to do, how not to treat people, what not to say. Also, whatever you do, don't allow the actions of other people to cause you to sin. Your love for God should be so much so, that you do not want to do anything to disappoint Him. No yelling or cursing them out. No talking behind their back or acting malicious. Besides, the satisfaction in doing those things are only temporary. Although you may have a sense of personal satisfaction for the moment, it won't really change anything for the better in the long run.

On the flip side, when you have someone that does something you do like, learn from that as well. Learn how to take that positive moment you experience and give it to someone else. Every experience should be a learning experience. One can never be too old to learn.

Every experience should be a learning experience. One can never be too old to learn.

I once heard my Pastor say something extremely profound. When situations come our way we have to learn how to respond and not react. Anyone can react, but it takes a strong person to respond. In your response, you must always remember to pray. Pray for others, but also pray for yourself. Also, above all else walk in love. While it's easy to point the finger, self-reflection can sometimes be a hard pill to swallow. My question to you, the next time you are faced with an unforeseen situation, how will you deal?

Life Tools:

Ephesians 4:29 NLT "Don't use foul or abusive language. Let everything you say be good and helpful, so that your words will be an encouragement to those who hear them."

Proverbs 21:23 KJV" Whoso keepeth his mouth and his tongue keepeth his soul from troubles."

FEAR HAS NO PLACE IN YOUR LIFE

What would you do, or even better what could you do if fear were not a factor in your life? Often times we put limitations and restrictions on ourselves, simply because we are afraid of what the results may be. We are afraid of failure. My question to you however, is what could you do or what would you do if failure was not an option? If you knew you could not fail, what is the very first task that you would embark upon to help you reach your destiny in life?

There are so many things that God has placed inside each and every one of us, and His desire is to see those things come to fruition. It is imperative that the children of God come out of bondage and stop allowing the enemy to cause us to fear. You must step up your faith to the next level. Trust and believe that even if you cannot see it, your trust in God is great enough that you will at least try. You will do your part and let God do the rest. In order to this however, you must cancel the spirit of fear daily. The opposite of fear is faith, so as you cancel fear you have to walk in faith. If God has placed something in your heart to do, do it. Start making provisions to get it done. Do some research, ask questions, come up with a strategy, just do it.

One thing I noticed is that when God places an idea in my mind, He does so in such a way that I know it is nobody but Him because I would have never come up with something like that on my own. As soon as He gives it to me though, the enemy will come right behind Him and try to cause me to doubt, giving me all kinds of reasons why it cannot be done. This is why I say we have to cancel the spirit of fear daily, and rebuke the devil. Once I began to call satan out for who he is, a liar it truly helped transform my ability to not only hear from God but respond to what He was telling me to do in obedience.

> If you truly believe that you can do all things through Christ, it is time for your beliefs to line up with your behavior.

If you truly believe that you can do all things through Christ, it is time for your beliefs to line up with your behavior. Here's my challenge to you, going back to the question I ask earlier. What is that one thing you would do if fear were not a factor? If you knew failure wasn't an option? If it's go back to school, I challenge you to contact no less than three schools that you are interested in and put in at least one application for enrollment. If you want to start your own business, I challenge you to come up with a name for your business, concept and slogan. Maybe it's find a job, I challenge you to update your resume, look up possible jobs that could work for you and put in at least one application.

Whatever your "thing" is, just do it. F.E.A.R is also known as False Evidence Appearing Real. Stop allowing the enemy to fill your head with false information and prevent you from walking in your destiny. The fear free you is the real you. Say these words, "I decree and declare that fear has no place in my life. I trust and believe that God has not given me a spirit of fear, but of power, love and a sound mind." Again, I'll end with this thought, what would you do if fear were not a factor?

Life Tools:

2 Timothy 1:7 KJV "For God hath not given us the spirit of fear; but of power, and of love, and of a sound mind."

1 John 4:18 NLT "Such love has no fear, because perfect love expels all fear. If we are afraid, it is for fear of punishment, and this shows that we have not fully experienced his perfect love."

YOU ARE NEVER ALONE

"The Lord was with him..." has been an ongoing theme in my studies for quite some time now. As I began to meditate more and more about what this really means, I decided to write about. Saved or not, here is a question I want to ask, do you believe that God is with you? If so, do you believe He's with you at all times? What does that mean for you? Because of the fact that this is something that has come up repeatedly, these are questions I had to seriously sit down and think about. I do believe and take solace in recognizing God's presence in my life. And I believe that He is ever present at all times, no matter what kind of situation I am in I can say with confidence and peace in my spirit that He is there.

I consider there to be many different answers to that last question in regards to what it means to me knowing that He's there, but success and favor are two that immediately come to mind. Favor is simply an attitude of approval or liking and to show approval and preference for someone or something. Achievement, victory, accomplishment and triumph are a few words synonymous with success. So based on my response and the definitions listed below, I think it is safe to say that if the Lord is with you at all times, success and favor are bound to be with you as well. But let's flip things up a bit, what about trials and tribulations? If you have trials and tribulations, any unwanted obstacles, situations or circumstances does that mean that God isn't with you? Absolutely not.

God being with us is a marvelous thing, and according to His word, He is most certainly with us at all times. This does not mean however, that everything will always be terrific or that there won't be any difficulties that you have to overcome. What you have to understand is that no matter how tough or bad it may feel, every time you come up against a hurdle, you have to jump over. Once you jump over, it will actually push you even further towards success, if and only if you allow it to. Remember, not only is the teacher quiet during a test, but the teacher is right there the entire time overlooking the class to make sure everything is done the right way. Now let me add this food for thought... many people think that when they are going through a test in life, God is trying to teach them something. Not so my friends! A good teacher does not use a test to teach you something. The test measures what you already know.

Success is effectiveness. It is also a state of mind. So as you take the good with the bad, do the thing you were created to do. Accomplish all that is within you. While doing so, trust and hold on to the fact that God is with you in all things. This will enable you to walk lucratively, with your head held high no matter what. God wants His children to be successful, victorious, triumphant and effective. It is just a process that you must go through to get there. While going through this process, you must always remember that no matter how isolated you feel you are never alone. God is always with you and His word declares that He will never leave you nor forsake you.

God wants His children to be successful, victorious, triumphant and effective. It is just a process that you must go through to get there.

Life Tools:

Genesis 39:2 KJV "And the Lord was with Joseph, and he was a prosperous man; and he was in the house of his master the Egyptian."

James 1:2-4NLT "Dear brothers and sisters, when troubles come your way, consider it an opportunity for great joy. For you know that when your faith is tested, your endurance has a chance to grow. So let it grow, for when your endurance is fully developed, you will be perfect and complete, needing nothing."

Deuteronomy 31:8 NIV "The LORD himself goes before you and will be with you; he will never leave you nor forsake you. Do not be afraid; do not be discouraged."

RAIN FALLS ON THE JUST AND UNJUST

It is never a good idea to look at someone while they are in a bad situation and just assume that they are doing something wrong. I have really come to learn that a lot of times folks don't want to share their story or truly open their heart to other people for just that reason. They make a decision not to reach out for help because in spite of the crazy situation going on at that time, they are more concerned about what other people are going to think of them, or if they are going to be judged. This rationale is why a lot of people feel like they have to go through things alone. Guess what, that is just where the enemy would want you to be. Satan wants to isolate you, because that is where you are more vulnerable. We must do our parts to make sure this does not happen. As children of God, our love and compassion for people must be unconditional and more importantly unrestricted. No matter what the situation is or the circumstances surrounding that situation, you must never judge or look down upon someone. You are to be a living, walking, talking, breathing, example of Him. This means having genuine compassion for people, more than ever, in their time of need.

If an individual confides in you, nine times out of ten that is God opening the door for you to be His vessel to operate in that individual's life. We must remember that God uses people all the time to get the job done. Count it not strange if that person comes to you. God could be placing you in a position which will allow you to show that person who He is. It could be for you to help, comfort, and give them the encouragement and support they need to get back on track. Put it like this, whatever their need is at the time, God could very well be using you to show Himself strong in their life.

Just like the alternating months throughout the year, everyone goes through different seasons in their life. While you are looking down on somebody else, be mindful that your season could be just around the corner. The word of God declares that the rain falls on the just and the unjust, so do not think just because you are saved or think you are living right that there won't be obstacles you have to overcome.

While reading this, you may be thinking to yourself that this does not really apply to you because you don't look down on people or judge anyone. Carefully think and have a serious time of self-reflection. Even if you have done it secretly or maybe even thought it in your mind and not said it, everything that has been said here can still apply to you because the fact of the matter is; it's still in your heart. Out of the abundance of the heart the mouth speaks, or sometimes thinks, but nevertheless it is still inside of you.

Pray and repent and ask God to help you. Acknowledging that the fault is there is first, but you have to understand that is it not something that you can change on your own. Only God can do it. Ask Him to help take those dark places out of your heart and replace it with His supernatural love and kindness for people. It is then that God will truly be able to use you, as we so often ask Him to do. You reap what you sow, and that biblical principle does not only apply to tangible things. If you treat people right, when problems come your way God will in turn send someone to you and allow you to reap that same love.

Life Tools:

Matthew 5:45 NLT "In that way, you will be acting as true children of your Father in heaven. For he gives his sunlight to both the evil and the good, and he sends rain on the just and the unjust alike."

James 4:12 NIV " There is only one Lawgiver and Judge, the one who is able to save and destroy. But you – who are you to judge your neighbor?"

KEEP IT REAL

One of the biggest problems with people, especially in the body of Christ in my opinion, are individuals who are fake and wear a facade to try and appear to be someone they really are not. This bothers me a great deal and I think it is important to identify and understand the real reason this sort of behavior takes place. There was once a time in my life while I was younger entering into adulthood, where I put up a smokescreen and pretended to be something I really wasn't. Whether or not anyone knew, I do not know if they did they never said anything to me about it. Nevertheless, I pretended to be something I was not, and I can say with an honest and open heart that the reason why I did this is because I was not happy with myself. I wasn't happy with where I was in life, so I figured if I made it appear as though my life was bigger and better than it really was, I could cover up all the hurt, pain and struggle that I was dealing with internally.

I remember one day, reading an article about the importance of understanding who you are in Christ. Learning that I am an heir of God and a joint heir with Jesus Christ, I am above only and not beneath, I am the head and not the tail. All of these things sound great, but the true revelation for me was that all of these good things were not just made up. They are actually in the Bible. This was huge for me at the time, because in spite of my mess I have always had a reverence and respect for the word of God.

Upon realizing this, I knew this was a word I truly needed to stand on and believe. When you believe in the word completely, no matter how many flaws you may have, the desire to make things up and pretend will not exist. It was at that moment when I found the ability to truly come to grips with myself by being completely transparent and pouring my heart out to God. You do not have to expose yourself to everyone. Talk to your creator. God delivered me. He changed my mindset about who I was in Him, which in turn changed my behavior. He can do the same for you. He took the desire out of my heart to pretend, and placed the desire in my heart for me to love me again, imperfections and all. To love all of me, no matter what the world standards appeared to be. To love me by letting go of my past, trusting Him that no matter how bad it seemed in my eyes it was all predestined to bring me into the individual I am today.

For folks who are not saved, I can understand them conforming to the things of the world, going along with the trends in an effort to mask what is hidden deep down inside. On the opposite end however, it seems as though this acting, is extremely prevalent in the Body of Christ. As the Body of Christ, we are supposed to reach those same people in the world I was just referring to and draw them in. How can we do that when instead of dealing with our own issues, we are busy condemning and looking down on people because they have on a tight dress or smell like alcohol? If we aren't turning up our noses, then we are doing everything we can to make them believe we are something we really are not. They don't even see Jesus in us because they're too busy trying to look beyond all the foolishness.

You can't be a reflection of God until you look in the mirror and take a true assessment of yourself first. Ask God to change whatever it is within you that is not like Him. He wants you to come into the knowledge of who you are in Him. How do you begin to know who you are in Him? Study your word. It's all written in the Bible. Once you study the word of God and see what it says for yourself, you must then believe it. Believe that there is a King in you. Believe that you are a royal priesthood. Believe that nothing, absolutely nothing can ever separate you from the love of God. Find your identity in Christ alone and you won't have to struggle with trying to be a counterfeit. You can focus on being the best you that you can be. You are a one of a kind original. Love you just the way you are. Your creator sure does.

Once you study the word of God and see what it says for yourself, you must then believe it.

Life Tools:

Deuteronomy 28:13 KJV" And the LORD shall make thee the head, and not the tail; and thou shalt be above only, and thou shalt not be beneath; if that thou hearken unto the commandments of the LORD thy God, which

I command thee this day, to observe and to do them:"

2 Corinthians 5:17 NKJV "So God created man in his own image, in the image of God created he him; male and female created he them."

TICK TOCK...TICK TOCK

Amazing how things can change at the drop of a dime, literally. If and when it does, one of the first things that come to mind is wishing we could have gotten that time back or wishing we could change the time we did have. Two of my closest friends lost their mother in a very short time period. This impacted me in a way that I could have never imagined. It was a major loss that really served as a reality check for me. I realize that there are many things that I take for granted, never truly accepting the fact that tomorrow is not promised. Having lost a parent a few years earlier, one would think I have gotten this concept down pact, especially how devastating that whole experience was for me. I guess in my healing and grieving process, I chose to overlook certain things instead of etch them in my heart and operate as such from now until the day I die.

I'd like to focus for a moment on time. What is time? A period, season, interval, era or stages along with a host of other words are synonymous. No matter how you describe it, time is truly one of the most, if not the most valuable thing on earth.

It is such a cherished and precious gift that God gives, and as we all know, it is irreplaceable. Once gone, you can never get it back. We hear people say often to use your time wisely, but it is not until you are able to fully comprehend just how valuable time is that you can truly apply this concept to your daily life. As mentioned earlier, experience is a good teacher. Even if it's not a death in the family per se, if you are a full time student in school, working a full time job and raising two children then I'm sure you are able to treasure and sincerely appreciate those special moments you do have.

No matter how you describe it, time is truly one of the most, if not the most valuable thing on earth.

One area that I was guilty in with regards to time was spending time with my husband. Prior to us having any children, when things were what we like to call "normal", typical day to day activities would tend to take precedence over a lot of how the household operated. If we happened to be home at the same time for dinner, then we ate together, if not no big deal. He worked and I worked, we were both just busy and we were fine with that. My perspective on this changed however when his work sent him away. My husband is in the military and his third deployment was truly an eye opener. This experience allowed me to fully understand the importance of treasuring every moment I have with him. Why? Because I know and will never forget what it is like to have that time taken away. Same goes if you have children. You know and appreciate each and every day of your child's life and all the precious milestones because they grow up so quickly.

> Doing the right thing at the wrong time is just as bad as doing the wrong thing or not doing anything at all.

The Bible reminds us in Ecclesiastes that there is a time and season for everything. Time is indispensable and so is timing. While I write about understanding the value of time, it is also just as important to recognize the proper moments and seasons in life as well. Your desire should be to live synchronized to God's timetable for your life. Doing the right thing at the wrong time is just as bad as doing the wrong thing or not doing anything at all. We have to be in tune with God's timing and operate when He says. If He tells you to do something, do not procrastinate because you only have a certain time frame in which to get it done. This is how you know you are in the will of God, but you are also effective in your assignment. One thing you can be sure of is seasons in life come and go, just like the four seasons of the earth. You must possess the ability to discern who, what, when and where so you can be effective in the time you are in. All in all, God is the giver of time so whatever you do be sure to include HIM. Give back at least a small portion of what He has given to you. Sometime throughout your day make an effort to spend time with God. Talk to Him, read the Bible, listen to a sermon. Do something that is going to keep you connected to the source. Time in precious, be sure to use it wisely.

Life Tools:

Ecclesiastes 3:1-8 NLT "There is a time for everything, and a season for every activity under the heavens: a time to be born and a time to die, a time to plant and a time to uproot, a time to kill and a time to heal, a time to tear down and a time to build, a time to weep and a time to laugh, a time to mourn and a time to dance, a time to scatter stones and a time to gather them, a time to embrace and a time to refrain from embracing, a time to search and a time to give up, a time to keep and a time to throw away, a time to tear and a time to mend, a time to be silent and a time to speak, a time to love and a time to hate, a time for war and a time for peace."

Ephesians 5:16-17 NIV "making the most of every opportunity, because the days are evil. Therefore do not be foolish, but understand what the Lord's will is."

NO LIMITS

Let's think for a moment. If you had to look at your life right now and establish a plan for how you were going to move forward in buying a house, what would you come up with? You might write down on a list that you want a three bedroom house, with two and a half baths, a two car garage and you want to spend no more than $150,000. Or another example may be you want a new job that is full time, have a good salary, with medical benefits, and flexible hours. It is not bad to establish a plan; in fact the examples listed are great for trying to draw up a strategy on how to get ahead in life.

> You have to understand that although it is good to lay out a blueprint for yourself, it is not good for you to put limitations on it. Simply put, there are no limits when it comes to the things of God and the people of God.

Here's the thing though, you have to understand that although it is good to lay out a blueprint for yourself, it is not good for you to put limitations on it. Simply put, there are no limits when it comes to the things of God and the people of God. While you want that 3 bedroom house, God could desire to bless you with a 6 bedroom house. Or, while you are still in an apartment paying rent every month thinking you could never afford to actually purchase a home or qualify for a mortgage loan, God is saying not only will I bless you so you can afford it, I will also restore and build up your credit rating. You want a full time job with good benefits working for someone else, when God could want you to have your own business.

Could it be that this is just how you have been programmed mentally? To always put parameters around whatever it is you are trying to do? If so, it is time to reprogram your thoughts and realize that when you put limits on any area of your present situation or future, you are putting limits on God.

How do you go about reprogramming your thoughts? You start by getting rid of the old way of doing things and try something new. The new way would first and foremost be to include God in the initial planning process. When the thought first develops in your mind, talk to Him about it. You can come up with a hundred things that you want, but ask God what He wants for you. As you make your plans, let Him know it is what you want but that you believe that if it is His will you can get even more.

When I first started writing, my desire was very simple. I wanted to share my thoughts with people all over the world. I have a passion for taking the word of God to all of the nations and I want Him to use me to do just that. Before doing it though, I had to really get in a place where I could hear from God. Not only hear from God, but be obedient to what He said. When you first make up in your mind to do something, sometimes starting can be the hardest part. I had to prepare myself both mentally and spiritually. I refused to put any limits on myself because I trust God. I trust that

When you limit your dreams and goals, you limit God. You limit what you believe Him to be capable of doing in all areas of your life.

He is able to do exceedingly, abundantly; above all I can ever begin to ask or think.

When you limit your dreams and goals, you limit God. You limit what you believe Him to be capable of doing in all areas of your life. My question to you is this. What is it that you are wanting? What are your goals? What are your dreams? If you don't have any, I challenge you to establish some in every area of your life (family, work, finances, health, etc). Now, when you come up with the answer to these questions, my next challenge to you is to include God! Talk to Him about all of it and take off any and all limitations. Make your goals the minimum and let God add the maximum.

Life Tools:

Ephesians 3:20 NKJV "Now to Him who is able to do exceedingly abundantly above all that we ask or think, according to the power that works in us"

Habakkuk 2:2 KJV "And the LORD answered me, and said, Write the vision, and make it plain upon tables, that he may run that readeth it."

THINK BIG

One revelation that God gave me is that not only should you take off any limits you have placed on Him, but He cannot do a great thing in a little mind. This really got me to thinking and I will pose this question to you as well. Is your mind vast enough to encompass greatness or are you so simple minded that you can't imagine anything beyond what you can see in the present moment? I know that I have great faith in God, which gives me the ability to see beyond my present situation but I can honestly say that I am working every day on expanding my thought process to see the greatness ahead. It can be tough when there is so much hurt, rejection, and disappointment around you. What I am trying to do is set all of that to the side. I know that these things have all been put there to push me towards that greatness I asked about, it's just a matter of staying focused and not allowing those rough patches to throw you off track.

What I have learned is that it is so important to understand that many things in your life are birthed in your mind. It develops as a thought, and then it is up to you to act on it. What the devil will do is try to counterattack those thoughts and cause you to doubt. He knows there is greatness in you and he wants to do everything he can to prevent them from actually manifesting. If he can shut you down by using someone to say something negative to you and bring hurt and disappointment, then that is what he will do. Often times, he will even use people that are close to you to do it. The unfortunate part is they may not even realize they are being used. The Bible tells us that the enemy comes to kill, steal and destroy and you better believe that he will do it any way he can.

> Is your mind vast enough to encompass greatness? Or are you so simple minded that you can't imagine anything beyond what you can see in the present moment?

When you get that small inkling in your mind to do something that you know can only come from God, you must act on it. Obedience is not only better than sacrifice; obedience is where you get your blessings. Operating in a spirit of obedience will take you so far because it will allow the gifts that you are operating in to make room for you. As a servant of the Lord, I want to operate in greatness. Not for myself, but so that the Kingdom of God can truly get glory out of my life. My prayer is that your desire will be the same. You are human and will most certainly make mistakes, but let's not allow your mistakes to prevent you from operating in greatness for your life.

I end with these two questions, what's on your mind? More importantly, what are you doing about it? It's time to start thinking big. They say the sky's the limit, but I beg to differ. In Christ, there are no limits.

Life Tools:

Proverbs 18:16 KJV "A man's gift maketh room for him, and bringeth him before great men."

1 Samuel 15:22 NLT "But Samuel replied, "What is more pleasing to the LORD: your burnt offerings and sacrifices or your obedience to his voice? Listen! Obedience is better than sacrifice, and submission is better than offering the fat of rams."

EXERCISE YOUR FAITH

Often times you offer words of encouragement to someone when they are in a tough situation by telling them the importance of having faith and trusting God. Yes, indeed faith is an important factor when faced with obstacles in life but let's take things a little deeper for a moment. Why not make faith your lifestyle? Live life in such a way that you are required to get out of your comfort zone and actually make an effort to exercise your faith on a daily basis. This theory is truly transformational when you think about it. If you exercised faith on a daily basis and made it a part of your lifestyle, you could be faced with a situation that would literally kill someone else, yet you would survive and do so with a completely different perspective.

> A part of exercising your faith is humbling yourself and acknowledging that you are absolutely nothing without God. Acknowledging that the gifts you do have come from Him and in order for you to use them you need His help.

This concept is especially important when it comes to

utilizing the gifts that God has placed on the inside of you. There are a lot of gifts that God has given His children. You are either not comfortable operating in those gifts or if you do operate in the gifts you don't do it for the glory of God. A part of exercising your faith is humbling yourself and acknowledging that you are absolutely nothing without God. Acknowledging that the gifts you do have come from Him and in order for you to use them you need His help. There must be faith in order to use what God has given you and when you do, it must always be for His glory.

How do you exercise your faith? Well, the best example I can give you is to compare it to the same thing you do to exercise your physical body. When you first start exercising, you start slow. You don't just jump up and run ten miles on day one. You start with maybe one mile then work your way up from there. That is the same thing you can do with your faith. Jesus said we are to have the faith of a mustard seed, and a mustard seed is extremely tiny, virtually impossible to see with the human eye. The same way that running a marathon builds your physical strength, exercising your faith grows your spiritual strength. Spiritual maturity will also come with spiritual strength and growth in your personal relationship with God.

See, to God, your life is a finished picture, beautifully painted on a canvas and He is watching parts of it unfold each and every day. It's your faith and ability to not just talk about it, but actually make it a lifestyle that is going to help complete that beautiful picture. Remember, He is Alpha and Omega, the beginning and the end. You were created to be a central part of the Kingdom and to be used in a vast way. Stop looking at your present situation as the end all, be all and exercise your faith. You have a future that God is trying to get you to, but in order to get there you have to make it through where you are right now. So right now, my challenge to you... Change your lifestyle, exercise your faith and watch it transform every area of your life.

Life Tools:

James 2:17 NKJV "Thus also faith by itself, if it does not have works, is dead."

Hebrews 11:1 NIV "Now faith is confidence in what we hope for and assurance about what we do not see."

FOCUSED AND DETERMINED

What does it mean to be focused and determined? When I think of focus, making something the center of interest or activity is what comes to mind. Determined is having made a firm decision and resolving not to change it. These are two concepts I feel we should all purpose in our hearts to live by. Is it easy? No, it's not easy at all. You have to have enough will power deep down inside of you to keep moving forward, no matter what. Stuff happens or as I like to say, life happens. When it does, often times it can catch you off guard. Little things here and there like you get sick; your car breaks down, the internet stops working. I call these distractions. If you are just breezing through life with no goals or ambition you do not have to worry about these simple disruptions. However when you are actually trying to stay focused and live on purpose, that's when all hell seems to break loose.

This is why when you find your purpose in life; you must make a firm decision that you are going to fulfill that purpose, no matter what. You have to make a solid resolution that you are in it to win it. A key element in being able to move forward with your decision is the ability to not sweat the small stuff. You have to learn how to pick and choose your battles. Certain things simply aren't worth your time or energy. Focus on only those things that are most important and leave the other stuff alone. They are simply a diversion meant to get you off course.

As an online college Instructor, one of the first things I tell my students when they start my class is to be prepared for any and everything. I suggest that they have a backup computer, back up internet access, work ahead to complete each week's assignment, just overall stay ahead of the game. The reason I encourage them to do this is because should anything happen, they will be prepared. Preparation is half the battle for successfully completing the course, which in turn will push them towards their goal of obtaining a college degree.

Whatever it is you have going on in life, let today be the day you decide to get focused and determined towards fulfilling the purpose and plans that lie ahead of you. I decree and declare on this day that God is planning to do something new in your life. Out with the old, let's focus on the new. Are you ready for it?

My challenge to you:

Don't focus on today's struggle, focus on tomorrow's victory.
Don't pray about a job, pray for a company.
Don't look for a way out; determine to find a way up!
You got this! Why? Because God's got you!
Just keep pressing forward!!!

Life Tools:

Proverbs 4:25 ESV "Let your eyes look directly forward, and your gaze be straight before you."

1 Corinthians 9:24 NLT "Don't you realize that in a race everyone runs, but only one person gets the prize? So run to win!"

Philippians 3:14 KJV I press toward the mark for the prize of the high calling of God in Christ Jesus.

ALWAYS GIVE THANKS

As you go about each day living life as you see fit, you must never forget to give thanks to the one who gives life. I am not just talking about giving thanks for the big things, like a brand new car I'm talking about giving thanks for everything including the things often taken for granted. Food, shelter, clothes on your back, clean air to breathe, all of these things. You must be thankful because we could be like other people who do not have these modest luxuries in life. I'm sure this is something you already know, but I think a lot of people either forget or just don't care because it is not right in front of your face.

Just recently, while over in Europe, someone came to my church that was from a different country. This man was not from Germany, nor was he American, but he understood the English language and because he saw the signs outside of the church he knew this was the place he could come to get help. Long story short, come to find out this man was homeless and had not eaten any food in three days. He was in our area looking for work and had been traveling all over Europe trying to find a job. So many things about my interaction with this man got me to thinking. To think I had nerve enough to complain about the cold and rain outside, when I have a home that is nice and warm and here this man is homeless. I got mad when I first moved here because I couldn't find the specific type of foods I like at the grocery store, when again I meet this grown man who hasn't eaten anything in the past 3 days. All I could do was pray and ask God to forgive me for having an ungrateful heart. Truthfully, the main reason I wanted to write about this is because it should not take you running into someone who is going through hard times to be grateful for what you have. I have since made it a point to thank God for all the many blessings He continues to bestow upon me. I do not want to take anything for granted and neither should you.

While you complain about eating chicken instead of steak, there is somebody who doesn't have food at all. While you are upset because you want a bigger house, somebody is sleeping in their car every night. It's time to wake up put things in perspective.

Be careful of the outlook and perspective you have on life when it comes to things like this. Circumstances change, people change, things change and at a moment's notice everything you are used to could be taken away from you. While you complain about eating chicken instead of steak, there is somebody who doesn't have food at all and while you are upset because you want a bigger house, somebody is sleeping in their car every night. It's time to wake up and put things into perspective. The reality is this, if it weren't for God's grace and mercy that is new each and every morning there is no telling where any of us would be. And the beautiful part about it is there is nothing you can do to earn it or deserve. That's just who God is. His love is truly unconditional.

Life Tools:

1 Thessalonians 5:18 KJV "In everything give thanks: for this is the will of God in Christ Jesus concerning you"

James 1:17 NIV "Every good and perfect gift is from above, coming down from the Father of the heavenly lights, who does not change like shifting shadows."

DIFFERENT PEOPLE/DIFFERENT PURPOSES

Isn't it amazing how when you talk to certain people they make you feel a certain kind of way, especially if you hold a bond with that person? I say that because I recently talked to one of my best friends, and talking to her really just gave me the kick start I needed and allowed me to refocus. It wasn't anything that she said in particular, it was just the fact that she knows me and has known me for so long. When talking to her I could really just be myself and enjoy every minute of the conversation. Then I think about when I talk to my husband, who really is my confidant. It's like God placed this man in my life for so many different reasons, and one of them is to help me figure out me. What I mean is I am a thinker. Often times I think about a lot of different things and my mind just gets all jumbled up. When I try to talk to an average person about it, they think I am silly because I am not able to fully express what I mean in a way that they will understand. With my husband however, when I talk to him, he always helps me put things into perspective. It seems as though the light bulb in my head just clicks on during our conversation and what I couldn't express to anyone else, now makes sense. Not only does it make sense to me, but he also understands. Now, when I talk to either one of my brothers, no matter what situation is going on around me or how good or bad I may feel they always bring such happiness to my spirit. It's like they know how to cheer me up and make me smile because they are so witty and funny. In my dealings with them, they also challenge me to be a better me, a better sister, a better wife, a better daughter, a better friend, just an overall better person.

I gave these examples to say this; different people have different purposes in your life. Initially, you may not know or understand why God has connected you to them. As time goes by, ultimately their purpose should be to help push you towards your purpose. That being said, quit trying to make folks a part of your life who aren't trying to help you get to your purpose. AND stop giving people a role in your life that they were never meant to play. Everyone cannot be your best friend, everyone cannot be your husband or wife, everyone cannot be your brother or sister, so don't expect them to act like it. Then turn around and get disappointed when they don't. That is only setting yourself up for failure. We have such high expectations for people, which many times is why we end up getting hurt. If you put people in the right place in your life, and deal with them from the right perspective it will save you a lot pain and heartache, and that's speaking from personal experience.

Stop trying to make folks a part of your life who are not trying to help you get to your purpose. Stop giving people a role in your life that they were never meant to play.

Now sometimes, you will have some bad experiences with people, but these people have purpose too. They help reveal what is inside of you and expose all the hidden dark places the enemy may try to use against you. Once these areas are exposed, you ask God to take them away so you can move forward. These bad experiences also should strengthen you. You just have to pray and ask God to help you discern who's who and what's what. If you ask, He will show you.

There comes a point in your life when you realize who matters, who never did, who won't anymore and who always will. So, do not worry about people from your past, there is a reason why they didn't make it to your future. And thank God for the new people He will send your way to help thrust you towards the destiny and greatness that you have on your life.

Life Tools:

Jeremiah 29:11 ESV "For I know the plans I have for you, declares the Lord, plans for welfare and not for evil, to give you a future and a hope."

John 15:16 ESV "You did not choose me, but I chose you and appointed you that you should go and bear fruit and that your fruit should abide, so that whatever you ask the Father in my name, he may give it to you."

IF HE DID IT BEFORE, HE CAN DO IT AGAIN

Some of the lyrics to one of my favorite songs simply say, 'If He did it before He can do it again.' Who is He you might ask? God of course. Your Heavenly Father is the same today, yesterday and forever more but it seems like so many people seem to forget that. As a part of ministry, I have seen God bless and deliver people out of crazy situations. Then those same people turn around and end up in another situation yet they act as if they have forgotten all about their previous victory. This has to change. You should learn from your mistakes in bad times, but you should also learn from your success in good times. For example, you are struggling a little financially and your mortgage is due, then out of nowhere you get a check in the mail. You know that was nobody but God that delivered you in your hardship. So, if the next month you start having more problems, you have to know that God is going to work that out for you also, whatever it is. If for no other reason just based on your previous experience.

If God did it once, you better believe He can and will do it again. He is the same God right now that He was back then. What God promises He delivers. Here's the deal though, you can have, actually you must have, complete and total confidence in who God is. Make it personal. Not only know who God is, but know who He is to you. Do not base your confidence on who He is to other people. You must know Him for yourself because your victory is not going to be based on your Pastor's relationship with God. It's not going to be based on your grandmother's relationship with God. Your victory is based on your relationship with God. It may not come the next day or when you want it to come. I encourage you however to remain patient and keep the faith because just as sure as you are His child, it is coming. No matter how impossible it may seem, or crazy everything may look, you have to take God at His word.

He promised in Deuteronomy 31:18 that He would never leave you nor forsake you. Be encouraged my sisters and brothers in Christ. When you go through a storm, remind yourself that this is not the first one you have been through and it probably won't be the last. Whatever you do, don't stop. Don't quit. You did not come this far just to be defeated so keep your head up. You got this. Why? Because as previous experiences have shown, God's got you!

I want you to think about this for a moment. Whether you are going through something at the present moment or not, think back to a situation that seemed absolutely impossible for you to overcome. One that you didn't have a clue how you were going to make it out of, or if you were ever going to make it out BUT you did. The same way that God bought you out then, He can do the same again and again and again. He is Alpha and Omega, the beginning and the end. He is the same God right now that He was back then.

Life Tools:

Deuteronomy 31:18 NLT "Do not be afraid or discouraged, for the LORD will personally go ahead of you. He will be with you; he will neither fail you nor abandon you."

Revelation 22:13 NIV "I am the Alpha and the Omega, the First and the Last, the Beginning and the End."

HE ALREADY KNOWS

When a problem arises in your life, you have to remember that God already had a plan for our breakthrough and victory over the situation prior to it ever happening. He is all seeing and all knowing, which means He is never surprised when the enemy attacks. Although you may feel caught off guard or taken back by the present situation, this is not so for God. He is never shocked or surprised trying to figure out what to do to help His children. As humans, a lot of times we get so caught up in our feelings or emotions, when we shouldn't. Instead we have to get up, shake the dust off our feet, and do our part. Make it personal, DO YOUR PART. Let God do the 'super' and you do the 'natural'. No matter what the situation is, you must never lose focus. Don't meditate on how big your problems are; take solace in how big your God is. If you focus on God and not the problem, you will see that He is so much bigger. How do you focus on God??? You worship Him, you praise Him, you love on Him, you serve Him with a spirit of obedience, and you spend time with Him. While doing this, you will begin to see the manifestation of His solution. This will also allow you to be in tune with His spirit so you can hear from Him clearly as He gives guidance and direction on how to move forward.

The element of surprise can be a good thing, but it can also be a bad thing. I can remember times in my life where I have been really shocked. One of the last times I can think of when I was shocked by someone, I prayed and asked God to never let me experience that again. I do believe that He heard my prayers because since then, I can honestly say that I have not felt that way. I learned how to pray the right way and began to cancel the assignment of the enemy to try and shock me or catch me off guard. Not to say that people haven't done crazy

> You will never be an exceptional person if you continue to combat only ordinary battles. Everything you are going through, surprise or no surprise is making you stronger and exceptionally into the unique, distinctive individual that God created you to be.

things, but God has always prepared me both mentally and spiritually on how to deal. And I believe that He will continue to do just that.

You will never be an exceptional person if you continue to combat only ordinary battles. Everything you are going through, surprise or no surprise is making you stronger and exceptionally into the unique, distinctive individual that God created you to be. Remember, God is not like man. He is never surprised because He already knows everything.

Life Tools:

Job 28:24 ESV "For he looks to the ends of the earth and sees everything under the heavens."

1 John 5:4 NAS "For whatever is born of God overcomes the world; and this is the victory that has overcome the world – our faith."

PERFECTION, IS THAT EVEN PRACTICAL?

Often times we strive for perfection in ourselves and even look for it in other people as well. The fact of the matter is that no one is perfect. We all make mistakes, and as the Bible states in Romans 3:23, we all have sinned and fall short of the glory of God. The only perfect person to ever walk this earth is Jesus Christ and that was a part of His purpose. He came to live a life of perfection so that He could be an example.

Here is something I want to just throw out there that I was thinking about. Is it possible to strive for perfection but not be saved and know Christ as your personal Lord and Savior? If you do not know Jesus who is the definition of perfection in my book, or believe in who He is, how will you know what you are striving for? Just a thought.

Nevertheless, when it comes to perfection do not beat yourself up or allow someone else to. Take every day one day at a time. If you slip up, learn from your mistakes and try again until you get it right. Once you figure it out, turn around and show someone else that same compassion.

I learned a while ago that it is not what you say to me that matters, it's what I say to me that matters. In other words, I have to find my own distinctive identity and be confident in who I am when I look at myself in the mirror every morning. In a real battle the battleground is always internal. It is easy to point the finger at other people. Doing this allows you to take the focus off yourself and put it on someone else.

Get to know your likes or dislikes, strengths, abilities and even your weaknesses. This way, when someone else decides to point out your imperfections or say what you can or cannot do, who you can or cannot be, you will have enough confidence and buoyancy inside of you to reject it.

While you are busy trying to figure out everyone else, it is important that you understand you. Be comfortable with you, love you. Get to know your likes or dislikes, strengths, abilities and even your weaknesses. This way, when someone else decides to point out your imperfections or say what you can or cannot do, who you can or cannot be, you will have enough confidence and buoyancy inside of you to reject it. Do not receive any negative seeds planted in your life. Most importantly you should be able to stand on the word and know that you may not be perfect, but you are a child of the King. You are an heir of God and a joint heir with Jesus Christ. You are the head and not the tail. Imperfections and all, no weapon formed against you shall prosper because you are more than a conqueror. Never let someone else define who you are!

Life Tools:

1 Peter 2: 21- 22 KJV "For even hereunto were you called: because Christ also suffered for us, leaving us an example, that you should follow his steps: Who did no sin, neither was guile found in his mouth:"

Colossians 3: 23-24 NLT "Work willingly at whatever you do, as though you were working for the Lord rather than for people. Remember that the Lord will give you an inheritance as your reward, and that the Master you are serving is Christ."

JUST ONE OF THOSE DAYS

Have you ever just woke up in the morning feeling like it was going to be 'just one of those days'? A day when you don't want to do anything but stay in bed. I have had a few days like this. For me, days like these sometimes give me an uneasy feeling in my spirit. My mind begins racing a hundred miles a minute thinking about everything and nothing all at the same time. As I get up and start moving, I pray. This gives me some peace, but the lingering feeling just doesn't really go away. By the grace of God, I make it through to the end of the day with this thought in my mind, I'll try again tomorrow. How do you handle days like these? Why do you even have them?

Although I am not a fan of days like these, I truly believe that God allows us to go through to shake some things up. What I mean by that is God is trying to change some things up. For instance, you may have a set schedule in regards to your prayer life or time that you spend with God. Sometimes you get so caught up in your routine that God wants to break up the regularity. He wants you to pray differently, read your word differently, just overall spend time with Him differently. I know at one point, there was a time in my life where I would use certain mornings as my in depth prayer time and study my Bible comprehensively on other mornings. Now, of course I would pray and study every day, but not as in depth as I did on these particular days. The Lord showed me that He wanted me to change things up a bit. In order for Him to get me to that next level, He had to modify my regular scheduled programming.

When there is transformation and growth taking place, you cannot continue to do the same old thing the same old way. If you do you will get the same old results. This can be said for everyday life, not just spiritually. The definition of insanity is doing the same thing expecting different results, hence where the uneasy feeling

When there is transformation and growth taking place, you cannot continue to do the same old thing the same old way. If you do you will get the same old results.

comes in. God is constantly growing and maturing you in Him. In order for that to happen, something's in your life and in your everyday 'norms' are going to have to shift.

As for how you handle when the shift is taking place, first and foremost you have to acknowledge it for what it is. When you get that feeling on the inside, but you aren't sure what's going on recognize the fact that there is indeed something going on. Don't just count it off as being tired or stressed. No, that is what the enemy would have you to believe. When those feelings come, talk to God. Not just because you know it's the right thing to do, be 100 percent honest with Him and tell Him how you feel. Be real with God. If you aren't fully transparent, then there is no way you're going to be able to make it through. Besides, He already knows anyway. When you express your feelings take a minute, and pause. Hear what He has to say back to you. He will then reveal to you what is happening so you can have a greater understanding of what is going on in your life.

It can be tough to experience days like what I've mentioned above. You must understand however that there is a bigger picture. So in reality, having 'just one of those days' could really be a great thing because it is evidence that a shift is taking place. Instead of feeling down and out, change your way of thinking. Ask God to fill you, shape you, mold you, and make you into the man or woman of God that He created you to be. If that means breaking up the monotony in your life, then so be it. There's a reason that God allows things to happen. Embrace it. Learn from it. After all, that's what living life is all about.

Life Tools:

Psalms 139: 23-24 KJV "Search me, O God, and know my heart: try me, and know my thoughts: And see if there be any wicked way in me, and lead me in the way everlasting."

2 Corinthians 3:18 KJV "But we all, with open face beholding as in a glass the glory of the Lord, are changed into the same image from glory to glory, even as by the Spirit of the Lord."

STOP TRYING TO DO IT ON YOUR OWN

Even the strongest people get tired at times but God's love, His power and His strength never diminish. He is never too preoccupied or too busy to help and listen. The word says that when we are weak that is when He is made strong. So in turn, His strength is the source of our strength. It is imperative however, that you look to the root of the problem. A lot of times when you are going through, the tasks and responsibility that you are carrying can become overwhelming because you are trying to do it alone. God never intended for it to be this way. He didn't bless us with a family or job or simply life in general for us to think that we had to bear the load all by ourselves. He is here to help. God knows you have bills that need to be paid. He knows your children need to eat every day. We have to pray and talk to God. Doing so is humbling yourself and letting Him know you cannot do it on your own. This opens up the opportunity for Him to come in and provide the help that you need. He already knows our mind-set but we must recognize it then ask that He take those feelings away and replace them with peace and assurance.

I have to point out one additional fact, even though God never intended for you to have to carry the weight of life on our own you have to discern how important decisions are. A decision is defined as a conclusion or resolution reached after consideration. Decisions have a direct impact on life. If you spend your rent money on a new outfit, then you can't turn around pray and ask God to bless you with a roof over your head. He already did that. You got what you wanted; now you are begging for what you need. That is backwards. Yes, God is here to help. You just have to be responsible and a good steward over what you have.

> Decisions have a direct impact on life. If you spend your rent money on new clothes, then you can't turn around and ask God to bless you with a roof over your head. He already did that. You got what you wanted; now you are begging for what you need. That is backwards.

Don't get it twisted my friends, God is your source. Just because you get a paycheck from your job every month, does not make them your source. Our Heavenly Father promises to provide, protect His children and never leave us. He will never, ever come short of His word. Let's be honest for a moment, even the best cars in the world can only run so far on a tank of gas. Eventually that car is going to have to be refilled before it can get back on the road. If you feel as though everything is going wrong and you can't make it any further, look to the source and trust that He's already working things out for your good. You are not alone, so stop trying to do everything on your own.

Life Tools:

Psalms 23 NLT "The LORD is my shepherd; I have all that I need. He lets me rest in green meadows; he leads me beside peaceful streams. He renews my strength. He guides me along right paths, bringing honor to his name. Even when I walk through the darkest valley, I will not be afraid, for you are close beside me. Your rod and your staff protect and comfort me. You prepare a feast for me in the presence of my enemies. You honor me by anointing my head with oil. My cup overflows with blessings. Surely your goodness and unfailing love will pursue me all the days of my life, and I will live in the house of the Lord *forever."*

IS THERE ANYTHING TOO HARD FOR GOD?

Is there anything too hard for God? This is something I have thought about quite a bit and the fact of the matter is, of course not. Think about it for a moment, sometimes you allow your problems, unwanted situations or circumstances to be as big as you are, which in your eyes I'm sure is pretty big. But truth is God, who created Heaven and Earth is so big that you can't even imagine. What may seem to be a big issue is not an issue at all to God. Why you might ask? Because He holds the whole world in His hands. He created the Universe, the stars, the sky, the trees, and the ocean. He created you. He created everything. He already knows what is going to happen before it ever transpires and He knows how you are going to handle it.

So if you know that nothing is too hard for God, why are you letting the issues and weight of the world hold you down? It is imperative that you get to that place in life where no matter what is happening around you, you establish and maintain a firm belief in the capability, strength, certainty, reliability, truth, and consistency of God and God alone. The capability of God supercedes that of any other because as the Bible declares, He has all power in His hands. His strength is far greater than you could ever imagine possible. The certainty of God is based on His word. You must study the word so you can know the word for yourself and in turn take God at His word. This way you can be certain that He will do what His word says. God is the definition of what reliable means. You can always rely on Him when no one else is around. He is the way, the truth and the light. He consistently shows us grace and mercy each and every day even though we don't deserve it.

> It is imperative that you get to that place in life where no matter what is happening around you, you establish and maintain a firm belief in the capability, strength, certainty, reliability, truth, and consistency of God and God alone.

With God, your troubles and dilemmas are never what they appear to be, but if you try to work it out the way you want to, it just may become exactly what it appears. Set yourself to the side for a minute, or as a dear friend of mine would say, stop trying to grow a brain. Just trust God. I think it's safe to say that for the most part, you trust people that you know. Could this be why it's so hard for you to trust God, because you don't really know Him? I encourage you right now to build a relationship with the architect of your life. Get to know Him. Spend time with Him. Then while you are going through the ups and downs of life, you will have the innate ability to see things totally different. You will be able to look to your creator first above all things and trust He's already working it out for your good and for His glory. So stop telling God how big your problems are, tell your problems how big your God is.

Life Tools:

Jeremiah 32:17 NLT ""O Sovereign LORD! You made the heavens and earth by your strong hand and powerful arm. Nothing is too hard for you!"

Jeremiah 32:27KJV "Behold, I am the LORD, the God of all flesh: is there anything too hard for me?"

TRAIN UP A CHILD

It seems as though things have gotten so out of control lately in regards to our youth. I by no means claim to be old, but this new generation of youth coming up seems to be such a new breed. They are doing things I never would have even imagined while growing up. Even worse, they seem to have no sense of fear. They don't fear their parents, they don't fear their teachers, they don't fear police, they definitely don't fear each other, they don't fear dying and most importantly they have no fear or reverence of God. As sad as this is, I cannot help but wonder why that is. Is it because of the way they were brought up? Not putting the blame on parents because I am one, but at some point someone has to take accountability for this behavior. I know I was very stubborn, and had a smart mouth growing up. My childhood friends will tell you, I stayed on punishment as a kid. In spite of all this however, my parents did lay a foundation for me. The Bible says in Proverbs 22:6 that we are to train up a child in the way they should go. From the time I was born until I moved out of my mother's house to go off to college at the age of 17, I went to church every Sunday. No ifs, ands or buts about it. Not only did I go, I was involved. I was in Sunday school, choir, and went to summer camp, vacation Bible school. Pretty much any and everything they had going on for the youth, I was a part of it. It may not have meant much to me then, in fact there were times that I hated going, but nevertheless the foundation was laid. Did I get wild and crazy when I went off to college, yeah I did some stuff I probably shouldn't have done, but I always had a reverence for God and who He is in my life. This element seems to be missing right now and it has to change.

If somebody breaks in your house and steals your money or any other precious possession, without a doubt you want it back don't you? Are our kids not more precious than money or any other tangible item? We have to take back our children. The enemy is out to kill, steal and destroy and if he is trying to use our children to do just that. We have to shut him down. He has infiltrated the hearts and minds of children through music, the internet, social media, video games, and several other means. I know this is a new century and we are a lot more technologically advanced, but that is no excuse. If your kids are online, know what they are doing. Put blocks on your internet, computers, TV's and anything else so you can prevent them from doing stuff when you are not around. You must pay attention. This brings me to my next thought.

You must make it a point to spend time with your children. I understand the responsibility of being an adult, let alone being a parent. This is no excuse however for not spending time with your children. A person can say they love you all day, but if they aren't spending any time with you, then what they say don't really mean a hill of beans. Make time out of your busy schedule for your children. If you have to, make an appointment with them just like you do your doctor. Take them to lunch, sit and play a game with them, go to a movie; do something that lets them know you are not focused on anything else at that time but spending time with them. If you do this you will build a closer relationship and your children will also become comfortable talking to you. They will see you as more than just the disciplinarian or the go to person when they need a new pair of shoes. It established a rapport and our youth need that. They need healthy relationships in their life.

Yes, indeed children will be children. I get that, but it seems as though that's part of the problem as well. Too many kids have been forced to grow up way too quickly. They have to play the role of an adult. In result, they are missing out on what being a child is all about. Being able to laugh and play, have nothing to worry about but going to school and get good grades. The times have truly changed. It is up to us to cancel the assignment of the devil and put him in his place. Command him to take his hands off our children. They belong to the most High God.

Tomorrow is not promised to anyone, no matter how young or old. It is essential that you cover your children with the blood of Jesus through prayer constantly. In addition to praying for them, you have to lay the foundation for them while they are young. Teach them about God, take them to church, teach them how to pray for themselves and how to build a personal relationship with God. You must also spend time with them and be an example. We cannot say one thing, then turn around and do something else. As I have learned lately, children hear what you say but they are actually moved more by what you do.

Life Tools:

Matthew 18:2-6 NLT "Jesus called a small child over to him and put the child among them. Then he said, "I assure you, unless you turn from your sins and become as little children, you will never get into the Kingdom of Heaven. Therefore, anyone who becomes as humble as this little child is the greatest in the Kingdom of Heaven. And anyone who welcomes a little child like this on my behalf is welcoming me. But if anyone causes one of these little ones who trusts in me to lose faith, it would be better for that person to be thrown into the sea with a large millstone tied around the neck."

*****I would like to invite every parent to pray this prayer over your children daily and do so out loud – release it into the atmosphere!*****

Father God in the name of Jesus, I come pleading the precious blood of Jesus over my children right now. I release their names into the atmosphere (say their names) and I decree and declare that spiritual intercessors all over the world are picking them up in the spirit. I plead the blood from the top of their head to the bottom of their feet. I draw a bloodline of protection around them allowing no incidents, accidents, situations or circumstances which will bring them any hurt harm or danger to come anywhere near them in Jesus name. Your word says that whatever we bind on earth is bound in heaven and whatever we loose on earth is loosed in heaven. I bind every plot, plan and scheme of the enemy to come against my children right now in the name of Jesus. I pull down strongholds and cast down vain imaginations. I dispatch warring angels to go before them and fight on their behalf. Fight against those that fight against them, war against those that war against them, in the mighty name of Jesus. I bind any spirits of oppression, depression, repression, suicide and bullying in the name of Jesus. I bind the spirit of anger or sorrow, low self-esteem, low self-worth right now in Jesus name. I release the perfect peace of God in their lives. The peace that surpasses all understanding. I release love, happiness and joy in their spirit. I decree and declare that they will live for you and serve you, the only true and living God all the days of their lives in Jesus name. No weapon formed against my children shall prosper and every tongue that rises against them in judgment I condemn right now in the name of Jesus. I decree and declare that they are an heir of God and a joint heir with Jesus Christ. I decree and declare that my children are the head and not the tail. They are above only and not beneath. My children are lenders and not borrowers. The wealth of the wicked is no longer stored up for them but is being released right now in Jesus name. I decree success, excellence and favor in the classrooms at school. My children will not conform to the ways of the world, they will not follow the standard, but they will be the standard in Jesus name. I thank you God for the new inventions and ideas that you have placed in their belly. I decree and declare that it will come forth in Jesus name. Success and progress are in their future. I cover their DNA with your DNA right now in the name of Jesus, and I decree and declare that they are healed, whole and complete in you God. I command sickness and disease to flee from their body right now in the name of Jesus. I decree and declare that they will live doubt free, drug free, debt free, disease free and drama free all the days of their life. I decree and declare that they will awaken each and every day ready to live the life of their dreams. Excellence will be the signature upon all they say and do. I seal this prayer in the matchless, magnificent, wonderful name of Jesus, Amen.

OPPORTUNITIES

I know several people made New Year's resolutions when the year first started. Stop doing this, start doing that, do more of this. I can be honest and say I didn't really make any resolutions for the New Year. I began 2013 with great expectations. I could not really pin point what those expectations were, so I did not specifically sit down and write a list. I just knew it in my spirit. I came into this year knowing that some things were about to change in my life for the good and I just needed to be ready when the opportunity presented itself.

What is an opportunity? I'd say it is pretty much when doors are opened or a set of circumstances fall into place that make it possible to do something. I believe that opportunities are around all the time, you just have to know when to take advantage. You cannot sit back and wait for them. Opportunities come in ways you don't even expect. If you are not ready for them, then it could just pass you by and you never even realize it. In my dialogue with people, I hear many different excuses and complaints as to why things aren't working out for them or how nothing seems to be falling in place as they had planned. Ok, so my question is this, how many times did an opportunity present itself but you let it pass you by because you were not ready?

Every gift, every talent and every skill that God gives you is an opportunity. Gifts, talents and skills all come from God. They are not something that can be earned or that you can buy. I also believe that the more you use the three of these (whatever they may be because they are different for every person), the more they grow.

Here is where I'd like to mentally separate the spiritual and natural things going on within, in order to gain a better understanding of how opportunities manifest themselves. Regardless of if an individual is saved, they are given a natural talent. That natural talent is usually the result of genetics and the surrounding environment. For instance, if you have a family history of musicians, more than likely you will be talented with music. Spiritual gifts on the other hand are given to all believers, people who are saved and have accepted Jesus Christ as their personal savior. As far as a skill, this is something you do well, simply put.

Now, think about your talents, gifts and skills. What are some opportunities that you may have missed out on and at the time didn't even realize it? Once you are able to identify what it is that God has placed on the inside of you, it begins that process for you to move forward and fully capitalize on the opportunities I've been talking about. Increase only happens when you learn how to discern the opportunities that God sends your way.

> Every gift, every talent and every skill that God gives you is an opportunity.

My prayer is that God will continue to help me discern these new opportunities and that I will trust Him enough to walk by faith and take total advantage of this new thing that He is doing in my life. I encourage you to do the same. Don't sit back and wait only to have new opportunities pass by. Get yourself together so that when those doors do open right in front of your eyes, you will be ready to walk right through in confidence.

My story may not be your story, but we all have a story. Purpose in your heart to make your story one that counts and one that will make a lasting impression not just for yourself, but for people all over the world. Are you a world changer? You can be! I challenge you today to be ready. Open your eyes and ears so when the next opportunity comes your way you will take full advantage, to the glory of God!

Life Tools:

Romans 12:3-8 NKJV "For I say, through the grace given to me, to everyone who is among you, not to think of himself more highly than he ought to think, but to think soberly, as God has dealt to each one a measure of faith. For as we have many members in one body, but all the members do not have the same function, so we, being many, are one body in Christ, and individually members of one another. Having then gifts differing according to the grace that is given to us, let us use them: if prophecy, let us prophesy in proportion to our faith; or ministry, let us use it in our ministering; he who teaches, in teaching; he who exhorts, in exhortation; he who gives, with liberality; he who leads, with diligence; he who shows mercy, with cheerfulness."

1 Corinthians 12:8-11 NKLV *"for to one is given the word of wisdom through the Spirit, to another the word of knowledge through the same Spirit, to another faith by the same Spirit, to another gifts of healings by the same Spirit, to another the working of miracles, to another prophecy, to another discerning of spirits, to another different kinds of tongues, to another the interpretation of tongues. But one and the same Spirit works all these things, distributing to each one individually as He wills."*

LET'S TALK ABOUT YOU

When someone asks the question who are you, at first thought it seems easy enough to give them your name or maybe where you're from. Simple enough right? Not so much. When asked who you are, if you truly think about it, it can be one of the most difficult and challenging questions for you to answer. I know for me, if someone asks me that question depending on who it is and the situation, I will more than likely go down a list; I am Nicole, I'm from Florida, I am a mother, I am a wife, I am a sister, I am a daughter, and the list could just go on and on and on. Nothing wrong with this list because it's the truth, I am all of these things. I have come to realize however that my life is so much deeper than that. This is why I can see how this question could be a lot more complex than it first appears.

Yes, you too could probably use a list of titles to describe who you are, but what about who you are deep down inside? What are you all about? Why on earth are you here? One revelation that God gave me while I was asking myself these questions was to shift my perspective a little on life. I will use this analogy to help explain. I'm sure that most of you have heard of a business having a mission statement. In fact, the mission statement is one of the first things established before the business can ever begin operating. The main goal of a mission statement for a business is to define the organizations purpose and primary objective. Its prime function however is internal. It brings the leadership together and helps them stay focused on the overall main goal, which for a company is to be successful.

Bring it back to you. Do you have your own personal mission statement? If not, before you do anything else you should write one. Doing so will help you a great deal as it relates to being able to identify your main purpose in life. As you create a mission statement, you will be able to pin point key areas of interest, areas that you maybe want to learn more about or grow in, as well as your strengths and weaknesses. What you think about, dream about, talk about, or actually do the most – this is what you are all about. These are the things that make you who you are. Or at least it should. This brings me to my last question I want you to think about. Does your life truly reflect what is important to you and how you want others to see you? In other words, if people on the outside looking in had to say what they thought seemed to be important to you, what would they say?

I know you don't do it often, but I want to you take a moment and think about you. I truly hope and pray that you are able to read this and do a little self-reflection. I only write about what I am thinking about and going through at the time and this is truly a time of self-reflection for me. I hear God telling me to be still and concentrate on me right now. Before I can successfully move forward I must do an internal investigation of myself to make sure me and God are on the same page.

I want to challenge you to follow suit and take a few moments for self-reflection. I say it's a challenge because if you are anything like me, you get so caught up in day to day activities so much so that you don't give yourself the time and attention you deserve. Today, God is saying be still. Establish your mission statement. What does your life reflect? Do you like it? If not, change it. If yes, keep doing what you are doing but look for ways to enhance it and make it better. You are you wherever you are, so be sure that you are the best you that you can possibly be. God Bless you.

Life Tools:

Philippians 2:5 NIV "In your relationships with one another, have the same mindset as Christ Jesus:"

Proverbs 16:9 ESV "The heart of man plans his way, but the LORD establishes his steps"

SEPARATION FROM THE NORM

As I've gotten older and experienced many aspects of life, I have come to realize that change is inevitable. A lot of times people are reluctant to change but what God has shown me is that in order to grow and mature, there may be times when He has to pull you away from the norm and change things up a bit. He does this to take you to a new dimension in Him. I like to think of it like this; God has to separate you in order to elevate you.

I remember a few years after I graduated from college, I got a new job and I was extremely excited about it. I was going to become a flight attendant. I'd be doing something I never even thought about doing, heck I had only been on an airplane once before even getting the job. But, deep down inside I knew this was the change I needed. What I didn't realize nonetheless was that I would have to leave everything I knew to take this job. I had to leave Florida, where all of my friends and family were located, and go up to Atlanta, Georgia. Now, technically for the job it was not required that I move, but between me and God it was a requirement. This was what He told me I had to do, so I did it. When I first moved to Georgia, I felt so alone and out of place, even though I loved my new job. What I had to realize was that God was separating me from my comfort zone. I had gotten so comfortable with the things, places and people around me. He was pulling me to a place where it would be just Him and I. A place where He could change and rearrange some things in my life that could have never happened had I stayed where I was.

When you are stretched out of your comfort zone or separated from the norm it can be a very testing, challenging and grueling experience. For me, it was all of the aforementioned plus some. But why is that? If we know that change is inevitable, why are we so reluctant? Why does it feel as though it is such a difficult journey? I know for me personally, the reason it was so tough is because I did not understand what was going on or why. We all desire understanding, especially in the midst of undesirable situations but there will be times when we just don't get it. The understanding comes after it is over and sometimes it never comes at all. That is like the clay trying to understand the potter while it's being molded into a vase or another beautiful piece of art, it just won't happen.

Separation brings elevation. Try not to focus on the situation while you are going through. Focus on what the outcome will be once it is over. I am here to tell you today, there is light at the end of the tunnel. You just gotta make your way through that tunnel full speed ahead with your eyes wide open so you can see the end. If you don't understand anything else, know that there is purpose behind any shift, change or alteration that comes your way. God is calling you higher, how will you respond?

Separation brings elevation. Try not to focus on the situation while you are going through. Focus on what the outcome will be once it is over.

Life Tools:

Ephesians 2:10 ESV "For we are his workmanship, created in Christ Jesus for good works, which God prepared beforehand, that we should walk in them."

Romans 12:2 NLT "Don't copy the behavior and customs of this world, but let God transform you into a new person by changing the way you think. Then you will learn to know God's will for you, which is good and pleasing and perfect."

GET A LIFE

What does your typical day consist of? Do you get up and go to work or maybe stay home and take care of your family? In the midst of all that you do for everyone else, do you actually have a life? What do you do for yourself? Having a job that you go to every day is understood and so is staying home to be a homemaker but if that is all your life consists of, we have a problem. So many people in my path seem to live lives that revolve around others. I used to be that same way until I realized that my loved ones and friends' lives should be a nice addition to my own. It should accent and compliment what I already love to do. This means that if they are not in the picture for one reason or another, I can still be content with doing me.

Prior to meeting my husband, this was something that God dealt with me on in regards to mates. It seemed as though when I would date someone, all of a sudden my life became immersed with whatever they had going on. I specifically remember praying and crying out to God one day and He said as clear as day, 'Get a

Life'. I was a bit taken back because I thought I had a life, but when I sat down and deliberated for a moment I realized God was right, I didn't. Yeah I went to work and even went to church and took an occasional shopping trip here and there, but that wasn't much of a life. I had to think about some things that I really loved to do, just for fun and do them.

My goal is to encourage you and really push you to go out there and have some fun. What is something you've always wanted to do but never got around to it? What's holding you back? I'll answer the second question for you, NOTHING. Go skydiving, ice skating, bungee jumping, white water kayaking, zip lining, travel the world! Whatever it is just do something. Life is too short to just stick to the same ole, same ole every day all day. That can be so boring.

An interesting piece that I wanted to add is directly related to the body of Christ. On numerous occasions I have ministered to people and talked salvation. One of the first things to come out of the persons mouth is that being saved looks boring. They don't feel like they can have a relationship with Jesus Christ, be saved, lived righteous and have fun all at the same time. I always laugh at this response because it couldn't be farther from the truth. The unfortunate part about it though is that this is the image that is projected by people in the church and who profess salvation all the time. Anytime somebody halfway talks about doing something that does not consist of reading your Bible, they want to look down upon or condemn folks. Let me first say this, nowhere in the Bible does it say that we have to read our Bibles all day every day.

My theory is this, examine your motives. I'm not going to look down on you. If you like to dance, do your thing cause so do I. Does that mean you have to be in the club dancing until three in the morning every Friday and Saturday night? Not so much. I had a blast when I was in the world, so I figure I'm gone do it even harder now that I'm saved. I just got a different partner. I'm rolling with Jesus now, so my approach is going to be a little more discrete. You might catch me in a dance class instead of in the club where the atmosphere is a little different.

Whatever your thing is, again I will say examine your motives. When you accept Jesus into your life as your personal savior and begin to have a true relationship with Him, your spirit will become more sensitive to things. There will be certain places and certain things you will not want to do anymore because you know that He is living inside of you. That being said, there are still lots of ways you can have fun and still be saved, many of which I listed earlier. Even if those things aren't of interest to you find something that is and do it. Have fun. Get out and do something different. Get A Life. You're worth it. And I promise you, God wouldn't want it any other way.

Life Tools:

John 10:10 KJV "The thief cometh not, but for to steal, and to kill, and to destroy: I am come that they might have life, and that they might have it more abundantly."

Psalms 118:17 NLT "I will not die; instead, I will live to tell what the LORD has done."

WE SHARE IN THIS HOUSE

Is it just me or do people seem to be stingy these days? I mean it just really seems like people are all about themselves and what they can get out of folks. This is one of the many things that seem to stick out to me now more than ever, not saying this doesn't happen everywhere, but it has just become more prevalent in my environment. Granted, there have been a lot of shifts and changes recently in my life. These changes have caused me to miss my family and friends a whole lot more. Plus, I am more of an introvert, so I keep to myself quite a bit. The people I do associate with are family or true friends I have had for quite a while. True enough, some friends and family will still use and abuse if you let them. For the most part however, I already know who operates like that, so I just love on them from a distance.

The law of reciprocity is vital in any functional relationship. There is give and take but it is not a one-way street, it comes from both ends. I remember studying a while ago about the different ways people love. In my studies, I was able to immediately pin point one of the characteristics that fit me perfectly, and that was a giver. I have no problems giving to people, in particular people who I have a relationship with. Over the years though, God has shown me that I have to be very discerning in my giving spirit because the enemy will try to use that as a means to attack. At first I didn't quite understand how the enemy could attack me in my giving, after all it was a choice I was making. The way the enemy moves is through people and what he will do is use people to try and take advantage of me. Let's be clear, I am not simply talking about physical things either. Yes, when you think of a typical gift it's something tangible, but tangible stuff doesn't mean all that much to me. It can easily be replaced. If I give you a new shirt, I can go buy a new shirt tomorrow to replace it, no big deal. I'm talking about giving as a whole. Giving your time, your attention, making sacrifices for people,

> The law of reciprocity is vital in any functional relationship. There is give and take but it is not a one-way street, it comes from both ends.

etc. All of the above is a form of giving because it requires you to take away from yourself.

Yes it hurts when I figure out that someone is only trying to get what they want out of me and I am sure it hurts you too. What bothers me even more is when someone does this to God. As a servant of God and active member in my church, I have seen many people simply use God. Now of course, this is just my take on the situation and I could be wrong. It just seems as though problem after problem people will come asking for this and that from God and as soon as they get what they want, they turn their back and walk away from Him. This makes me so angry. How could you do God like that? He is your daddy, your Heavenly Father who loves you so much. Yet you only come to Him when you want something or when you are going through a tough time.

As a parent, I can only imagine how this would make me feel. The crazy part about it is God is such a loving, gracious and merciful God. He knows what you are going to do and how you are going to do it. Yet He still allows you to walk around His earth breathing in His air, eat His food, have a roof over your head not to mention all the other things you take for granted. The law of reciprocity should not only be applied towards other individuals, it should be applied towards God as well.

I don't have to ask what He's done for you, but I will ask what have you done for Him lately? God is God, so there really isn't much you can do for Him anyway, but you can pray and talk to Him, you can spend time with Him, you can tell other people about Him. When you go to a restaurant that you like you tell people about it don't you? Well why not tell people about God? Isn't He a good God? Overall, you should at least do your best to have a true reciprocal relationship with Him.

It's funny because while God placed this on my hear to write about, I keep hearing my four year old daughter in the back of my head saying, "we share in this house". That is what her dad and I taught her when we had her baby sister so they can learn to share with one another. One of the best things about having children is that you can lay the foundation early and teach them how to share. I want my babies to know how to have a reciprocal relationship with each other and with people. I also hope and pray that they teach their children to do the same. God has been too good to us to just take, take, take and not want to give anything back in return. Count your blessings, then start passing them out to others, I know I will. After all, my baby girl said it best, "we share in this house".

Life Tools:

Hebrews 13:16 NIV "And do not forget to do good and to share with others, for with such sacrifices God is pleased."

1 Timothy 6:18 NLT "Tell them to use their money to do good. They should be rich in good works and generous to those in need, always being ready to share with others."

DARE TO BE DIFFERENT

I used to be called different all the time growing up and would really get offended by it. Why you talk like that? Why you act like that? Why you do this? Why you do that? It offended me because I didn't understand how I was different. Then of course as I got older I began to realize that the reality is, nine times out of ten everyone has a diverse perception of what ordinary is. I was different because I was supposed to be. Why do folks want other people to act like them, talk like them, and think like them? And when they don't, you consider them to be weird. You've got to stop trying to put people in a box. Everyone else will not conform to your little container of what you think is right or wrong or how you think it should be done. It is also important to learn how to respect one another's differences. We are all unique and special in our own way, so learn to embrace it. It is so sad now how our kids and even some adults look at so called "celebrities" and mimic what they see. Why? They put their pants on one leg at a time just like you. Instead of trying to fit in, you set the standard.

The Bible says that we are fearfully and wonderfully made. If you know that you are fearfully and wonderfully made, why not accept you? Don't try to fit in and conform to what everyone else is doing. Some folks just won't be able to handle you and that's fine. If they cannot handle you, then you do not need them in your circle anyway so keep it moving. If they talk about you, so what. I look at it like this; haters are confirmation to me that I am doing the right thing. So when they talk consider it a compliment. Let their negative words push you even further along your journey. Look at Jesus. Think about how they talked about Him and treated Him because He was different. He was different to them because He was love. He was not concerned about rules or religion. He was concerned about the heart of man. People at that time had never met anyone like Him. We are created in the image of God. So guess what that means, if He went through you better believe you will too.

Dare to be different. Follow the crown and not the crowd.

Dare to be different. Follow the crown and not the crowd. Jesus wasn't trying to be like everyone else. He came to show people a new way of life. As you live for Christ, there is no way you will be able to do so acting like everyone else. The more I get to know me and love me, the more I realize just how different I am and I love it. I have come to realize that there will never be another me, ever. Likewise, there will never be another you, ever. I am here to encourage you today to be different, I dare you. Be the greatest irreplaceable, exceptional, matchless you that you can be. Embrace you. Adore you. Love you, because God sure does.

Life Tools:

Psalms 139:14 NLT "Thank you for making me so wonderfully complex! Your workmanship is marvelous – how well I know it.

Romans 12:2 NLT "Don't copy the behavior and customs of this world, but let God transform you into a new person by changing the way you think. Then you will learn to know God's will for you, which is good and pleasing and perfect."

YOUR WORD IS YOUR BOND

There was a time when a person gave their word, one could be certain that the promise would be kept. Now and days it just seems as though people say one thing and five minutes later turn around and do something else. The part about it that is even worse is that they have no conviction about it. Whatever happened to your word being your bond? Why does it seem so hard to just do the right thing and have some integrity? Integrity is something that is proven over time by your behavior. In my opinion, it is a reputation of trustworthiness. When you say you are going to do it, then do it and if you can't be man or woman enough to say it. Even better, simply think about what you say before you say it so that you are not making a commitment you cannot fulfill. Do not be afraid to take a moment to think before answering a question. Use wisdom. I had to learn to do this because on multiple occasions I put myself in situations by saying something with good intentions, but when it came time to actually fulfill that commitment it was a lot more than I had anticipated. You have to get to a place of individual accountability and take responsibility for not only your actions or lack thereof, but your words as well.

Here is something to think about, when folks have a good talk game, which is what I like to call it because they know how to run their mouth very well, but their deeds do not line up that eventually leads to a lie. Thus, making the person who did not keep their word and do what they said they were going to do a liar. Just a friendly reminder, a liar is a person who is not honest and cannot be trusted because they do not speak with truth out of their mouth. No one likes to be called a liar. One must understand however that lying is not just when someone asks you something and you answer with a false response. Lying is saying you are going to do something and never do. Every time you go back on your word, the value of what you say decreases. Here

You have to get to a place of individual accountability and take responsibility for not only your actions or lack thereof, but your words as well.

is where that integrity I was talking about earlier comes in. If not for you, have enough respect and reverence for God. He sees all and knows all, so if you love Him and don't want to disappoint Him, think twice before you communicate so you don't disappoint your creator. I leave you with this, what is your word worth? Is your word truly your bond?

Life Tools:

Proverbs 12:22 NIV "The LORD detests lying lips, but he delights in people who are trustworthy."

Ephesians 4:29 ESV "Let no corrupting talk come out of your mouths, but only such as is good for building up, as fits the occasion, that it may give grace to those who hear."

Ecclesiastes 7:1KJV "A good name is better than precious ointment; and the day of death than the day of one's birth."

I WON'T COMPLAIN

Life is a whirlwind of both good and bad, highs and lows. You will have some great moments at times and you will have some not so great moments. The kicker is how will you handle these highs and lows, good or bad? For me, no matter what life may throw in my direction I choose not to complain. I made a conscience decision. This is a choice that I am sticking to. Have you ever known someone where every time you saw them they had something to complain about? If you ask them how they are doing, they go down a long list of stuff that is wrong with them. My toe hurt, my head hurt, my knee acting up... I mean something is always wrong. Personally, I try to avoid people like this. If I can't avoid them, I just say hello and try to make our interaction as brief as possible. I do not make small talk or anything because I don't want to hear their list of complaints about life, and I know they will have one. It's sad it has to be that way but their negativity begins to rub off after a while and I don't want it rubbing off on me. These types of people make the choice to focus on the negative and complain, instead of focusing on the positive. If your toe, knee and head hurt then thank God you still have your arms, hands and fingers that work just fine.

There is always a positive for every negative in your life. You just have to choose what side you are going to focus on. I think by focusing on the positive in your life, you also honor God. You let Him know that in spite of what situation or circumstance may be going on, you are still thankful for the many blessings that you do have. By maintaining a positive outlook, you show Him that you are able to see beyond the present chaos to the beautiful panorama that lies ahead.

There is always a positive for every negative in your life. You just have to choose what side you are going to focus on.

This in essence is what exercising faith is all about. Being able to praise God in advance and know that your present situation is only temporary. My charge to you is to make a conscience decision not to complain. If your whole body is aching, thank God that you are still breathing. If the worker in the store treats you horribly while shopping, instead of filing a complaint with the manager find someone who treats you the way you deserve to be treated and compliment them. Replace every complaint you have with a kind word instead. There is always good in every situation, you just have to find it.

Life Tools:

Philippians 4:8 NIV "Finally, brothers and sisters, whatever is true, whatever is noble, whatever is right, whatever is pure, whatever is lovely, whatever is admirable – if anything is excellent or praiseworthy – think about such things."

Proverbs 17:22 NLT "A cheerful heart is good medicine, but a broken spirit saps a person's strength."

STAY IN YOUR LANE

It's amazing to know that God has blessed each and every one of us with our own gifts and talents. Some people work great with children, some are very organized and do outstanding at administrative and clerical positions; others are very social and work well with other people. The list goes on and on because we are all such a diverse group of people. God made us this way and that's a beautiful thing. The issue I'd like to discuss however is about people not necessarily doing what they've been graced to do. Instead they do what they want to do.

If people would focus on themselves and what's ahead of them instead of getting caught up in all the craziness and confusion with what's going on around them life would go so much smoother. I don't go bowling often, but I do like to go every now and then because it is a lot of fun. When I bowl, I have learned that I don't do well if I am distracted by the activities happening around me on the other lanes. When it's my turn, I walk up to my lane, focus on the pins ahead of me, think about what I can do to knock them down then roll the ball. I am not fancy, no twists and twirls like some people because that does not work for me. If I try and do all of that I may end up hurting myself, literally. But no, what does not work for me works really well for professionals and I am fine with that. I said all of that to say this, make it a point to focus on your own strengths and abilities that God has placed on the inside of you. It is ok to have fun trying new things every now and then, but even when you do that do what works for you.

This concept is prevalent in so many areas of life. In marriages, family structures, even on our jobs. A husband and wife should be a team and work together as a team to make their marriage work. Marriages take a lot of work, dedication and of course focus by both people. To be successful, the husband must stay in his lane and do what a husband is supposed to do and a wife must stay in her lane and do what a wife is supposed to do. When you add children into the element, they also have a role to play in regards to the structure of the household. In most jobs, before you even applied for the position you knew what the specific job duties were.

This same theory is applied to the body of Christ as well. The word declares in 1 Corinthians 12 that the human body has many parts but all the parts still only make up one body. My legs cannot do what my eyes do and my stomach cannot do what my arms do. All different parts have their own specific duty in order for the body to function all together as a whole. God has gifted each of us to play a certain role in the church. When everyone gets on one accord and operates in their gift there is such an outpour of the spirit of God. His presence is strong and this sets an atmosphere of deliverance, break through, healing, salvation, just an overall manifestation of the glory of God. This is what God created the church to be all about.

You must become skilled at staying on the path that God has laid before you.

Why is it so easy to get distracted and get pulled out of your lane? As I said earlier, you get caught up in not so much doing what you know you should be doing but instead doing what you want to do, which nine times out of ten is going to be something you are comfortable with. This totally throws you off course. You must become skilled at staying on the path that God has laid before you. If you get knocked off for some reason, jump back on, dust your hands and feet off and continue to move forward.

At this point in my life, I am all about progress. I will not, to be perfectly honest; I cannot allow anything or anyone to get me off track. Successful people never worry about what other people are doing. They have enough going on in their own life. That's the place I'm at now. I have so much going on in my life, some might think too much. I am focused and determined to stay in my own lane so that I can reach the place that God has called me to. I am determined to leave behind a legacy not just for my children but also for my children's, children's, children all throughout my bloodline. Stay in your lane and see how far it takes you.

Life Tools:

1 Corinthians 12:12 NLT "The human body has many parts, but the many parts make up one whole body. So it is with the body of Christ."

Romans 12:3-5 NIV "For by the grace given me I say to every one of you: Do not think of yourself more highly than you ought, but rather think of yourself with sober judgment, in accordance with the faith God has distributed to each of you. For just as each of us has one body with many members, and these members do not all have the same function, so in Christ we, though many, form one body, and each member belongs to all the others."

THE TALK

One of the things that I am most passionate about in this Christian journey is getting people to understand prayer. Prayer is so powerful. It is life changing, and most importantly it is our direct line of communication with God. Communication is essentially the foundation for any relationship. I know you've seen people pray many different ways, what I've learned is that there is nothing wrong with that because there is really no set way of praying. Some like to scream and shout, others may be soft spoken or whisper and some prayers may even be in your head. Whichever method you prefer is fine because God hears them all. Right now, I don't want to focus so much on the method. I want to focus on the necessity.

For those who have children, think about how talking to your children makes you feel. It builds your relationship. True enough you want to make decisions for them that will help them and not hurt them, but you also want to see where their head is. You want to know where they are coming from. Communicating with your children strengthens the foundation and love that you have for one another. If you know that God is your Heavenly Father, how do you think He feels when His children communicate with Him? He feels the same way.

When you talk to God, it builds your relationship. It helps you grow spiritually and you are able to learn more and more about Him. When you pray that is when things begin to change. Prayer changes people, then people change things. Through prayer God equips and empowers you to do His bidding throughout the world.

As you gain more and more knowledge about prayer, the more you should want to do it. Life brings hardships and suffering it also brings joy and happiness. Either way, having a direct connection to your creator is a privilege. It is a privilege that you probably don't take advantage of nearly as much as you should. It is also an advantage. Being able to go directly to the source instead of worrying, or concerning yourself with the strange possibilities of life is a great benefit to being saved and communing with God. Prayer is an opportunity to humble yourself and worship God in a way that no other creature on this earth ever can.

One interesting fact that I'd like to leave you with is that the only thing the disciples asked Jesus to teach them to do was to pray. They must have understood and seen first-hand the power and significance in prayer and they wanted to know how to do it too. Before you do anything else, after reading this I want you to have 'The Talk' with God. If nothing else, tell Him thank you. Try it and I guarantee you'll love how you feel afterwards. Praying to your Heavenly Father will not hurt you. Not only will you find peace in talking to Him, the more you do it, the more you will feel His presence in your life. You will feel love because God is love. So go ahead and have 'The Talk', it is way overdue.

> Life brings hardships and suffering it also brings joy and happiness. Either way, having a direct connection to your creator is a privilege. It is a privilege that you probably don't take advantage of nearly as much as you should.

Life Tools:

Matthew 7:7-8 NIV "Ask and it will be given to you; seek and you will find; knock and the door will be opened to you. For everyone who asks receives; the one who seeks finds; and to the one who knocks, the door will be opened."

Luke 11:1-4 NKJV "Now it came to pass, as He was praying in a certain place, when He ceased, that one of His disciples said to Him, "Lord, teach us to pray, as John also taught his disciples." So He said to them, "When you pray, say: Our Father in heaven, Hallowed be Your name. Your kingdom come. Your will be done On earth as it is in heaven. Give us day by day our daily bread. And forgive us our sins, For we also forgive everyone who is indebted to us. And do not lead us into temptation, But deliver us from the evil one."

THE PERFECT TRANSFER

Every good conversation has at least two people both being able to express their thoughts and opinions right? Well, I previously went into the importance of prayer and how it is essential that you take time to talk to God. An element that cannot be left out however, is the ability to listen. This is how the perfect transfer takes place. In order for communication to be fully effective, you have to be able to not only talk but listen. Both parties involved have to communicate with one another.

God has so much to say to you if you would only be still for a moment and hear. I've been guilty on many occasions of pouring my heart out to God in prayer, then when I finish saying what I have to say I immediately go right back to doing whatever it was I was doing. Wrong. God could have answered what I was praying about right then, but I did not stay still long enough to hear Him. Now that I know better I do better, but I have to be honest because I still don't take the time to listen like I should.

The good thing about communicating with God is that He speaks in so many different ways. Sometimes He speaks in a small voice within, but this is not the only way He talks to us. If you are riding down the street He may talk to you through a billboard or poster. He also speaks through songs, through the word of God and sometimes He speaks through other people.

The location where the transfer takes place does not matter. You can pray in your kitchen while washing dishes, in the bathroom or simply lying in your bed. God is with you at all times, wherever you are. He is just waiting for you to acknowledge His presence. When you talk to Him you do just that. I named this 'The Perfect Transfer' because in whole that is what prayer is. You transfer information to God; He transfers information back to you. It should be a reciprocal exchange. So now the next thing I want you to do is when you pray, after you have said what you want to say take time to be still and quiet. Hear what God has to say to you. This is how you have the perfect transfer.

Life Tools:

Revelation 3:22 NLT "Anyone with ears to hear must listen to the Spirit and understand what he is saying to the churches."

Jeremiah 7:23 ESV "But this command I gave them: 'Obey my voice, and I will be your God, and you shall be my people.

And walk in all the way that I command you, that it may be well with you."

STUDY! RESEARCH! APPLY!

I can recall being a student in grade school and not having to study a whole lot to do well in class. Then as the years went on I was placed in classes that were a bit tougher. The ability to excel became more challenging. I talked to my mom about my difficulties and the first thing she asked me was did I study? Well, no not really because I never really had to study before. She reminded me that I was now working on a higher and more advanced level. In order for me to succeed like I had in the past it was going to take a little more effort and dedication. In other words, I was going to have to study. I was going to have to make a conscious effort to open up my books, read them, take notes and commit to memory the material. Then I would need to apply everything I learned to complete my tests and other assignments in class. This revelation changed my mindset on so many different levels. It was then that I realized at a young age, in order for me to get something I had never gotten I had to do something I had never done. I had never dealt with work on such a high level, so therefore the effort I was giving in the past was no longer sufficient. If I was going to get out of the class what I expected to get, a few adjustments were going to have to be made.

Now let's step out of the classroom for a moment. God is trying to do the same thing in your life. As you grow in Him more and more, there are going to be some thing's that have to change. You are not going to be able to overcome the trials and tribulations of life by keeping the same routine day-by-day, month-by-month, year-by-year. God is calling you higher and an essential tool that is going to get you where He is taking you is going to be us opening up the book. Not just opening it up, because anybody can do that, but actually reading and mediating on it. The Bible is God's written instruction manual on life. It provides light to avoid pitfalls in the path of life. Every situation you could possibly think of is in the Bible. This is why God desires for you to familiarize yourself with His word. It is not until you are able to fully appreciate it, will you be able to act upon it.

If there is something you do not understand while studying, research it. Ask questions, look it up online, read books do whatever you need to do until you get your answers. You have been blessed with new age technology so you have several tools available that will help you discover the meaning of anything you are not able to comprehend. I love to read books, so research does not bother me. I actually enjoy finding something in the Bible I don't understand because when I have to look it up I usually learn so much more than I would have expected. I love how God has gifted people all over the world to write books today, just as He did in the Bible days.

Once you get what you are reading and have the understanding you desire, you must then apply it. In order to be effective, this is what God is looking for. As you learn about the word of God, you learn more about Him. Then you should be able to apply what you have learned to your lives. Apply it to your character. Apply it to your personality. Apply it to your behavior. There's a word that comes along with application and it's called transformation.

Reading the Bible will do just that. It will transform you. Studying the word allows you to draw closer to God. Learning the word teaches you how to live a Godly life. With the help of the

Holy Spirit you also become equipped when you study the word. Equipped with what? Equipped with the tools needed to overcome the enemy. The enemy's job is the kill, steal and destroy and you better believe he is going to be on his job whether you are in your word of not. He does not want you to use your weapon, i.e. the Bible. Because he knows that as you take the time to get in your word the stronger you become. The stronger you are, the more likely you will be to put the devil in his place and walk in the victory that God has already given you.

As you take the time to get in your word the stronger you become. The stronger you are, the more likely you will be to put the devil in his place and walk in the victory that God has already given you.

Just so you know, you are held responsible for what you know. As you learn and investigate the word of God you will be expected to do better. The book of James tells us specifically that 'if we know good then we ought to do it and if we do not do it, it is a sin'. In other words, if you learn the word but keep doing whatever you want to do, however you want to do it, with whomever you want to do it with, then you are operating in sin.

Apply the word of God to your heart and to your life. You will have a makeover take place right before your eyes and you might not even know it. God is not expecting you to do anything on your own, never forget that. In this whole process, He will be right there with you. He loves you just that much. He knows that this life is not easy and He just wants to give you what you need so that you can make it through to live a life of eternal salvation.

Life Tools:

2 Timothy 2:15 KJV "Study to shew thyself approved unto God, a workman that needeth not to be ashamed, rightly dividing the word of truth."

Psalms 119:11 NLT "I have hidden your word in my heart, that I might not sin against you."

WISDOM IS AVAILABLE TO YOU

When you think about wisdom what is the first thing that comes to mind? For me it's usually an elderly person. I know that not all elderly people are wise, but most are. I also know you don't have to be old to be wise. Wisdom is something that can contribute to your sense of well-being and overall life satisfaction. It develops across your lifetime based on the experiences you have lived. Wisdom in every area of your life is a trait that you should aspire to achieve. What to do, when to do it, how to do it, etc. Not saying that if you make some wrong decisions you don't have wisdom. I'm saying that as you attain wisdom you will be better at making decisions. Truthfully speaking, when you make choices that maybe aren't so wise those are some of the best opportunities to learn.

Wisdom is truly a gift from God and the best way to get it is to ask. That seems simple enough right? Yet, how many people actually ask God for wisdom? You can also surround yourself with wise people. As the saying goes, 'you are the company you keep' and I truly believe this to be true. Those around you are a direct reflection of you. Even if you aren't doing the same thing when someone associates you with that person they will likewise associate your behavior. I love being around people who I can learn from. There are certain things in life I don't want to have to go through and if I can learn from someone else's mistakes then I want to do just that. I also thank God when He gives me the opportunity to share what I have been through with other people in hopes that they do not have to go through the same things I did.

Wisdom is a gift that is foundational to the church and it is clearly taught in the word of God. I always find it so powerful in the book of 1 Kings when God asked Solomon what he wanted. Solomon could have requested anything in the world but his desire was that he might attain wisdom. At his young age, he knew that by having wisdom it would help him to fulfill his destiny. The task that had been set before him as king was clearly not an easy one. He could have easily asked for God to take the burden away and give it to someone else. Let's bring it back home for a minute, how often do we run from what

God is telling us to do or ask Him to give that duty to someone else?

When God has given you a big responsibility ask Him to give you the wherewithal to fulfill that responsibility. You should not ask God to do for you what He wants to do through you. Instead, ask Him for the wisdom to know what to do and the courage to follow through on it. Wisdom is both the ability to discern what is best and the strength of character to act upon that knowledge. I also love using Solomon as an example, because yes he asked for wisdom, but there were some areas in his life where he did not act wise at all. You must know how to apply the wisdom that God gives.

Wisdom is only effective when it is put into action. This is an important element for the Body of Christ to recognize. Having experience, knowledge and good judgment will help you to love God even more, but you must in turn put that love into action. This will allow you to contribute tremendously to the church, which is the bride of Christ. Also, when you apply the wisdom that God gives to your life overall, you will be able to reach those outside of the church as well. Your love and the example you set by your actions will be another way of showing unbelievers what it means to be saved and attract them to Christ. Wisdom is available to you. If you haven't already, I encourage you to ask God for it. It is a gift that He desires to give you. He's just waiting for you to make your request known.

Life Tools:

Ephesians 1:17 NLT "Asking God, the glorious Father of our Lord Jesus Christ, to give you spiritual wisdom and insight so that you might grow in your knowledge of God."

James 1:5-6 NIV "If any of you lacks wisdom, you should ask God, who gives generously to all without finding fault, and it will be given to you. But when you ask, you must believe and not doubt, because the one who doubts is like a wave of the sea, blown and tossed by the wind."

1 Kings 3:5-12 NIV " At Gibeon the LORD appeared to Solomon during the night in a dream, and God said, "Ask for whatever you want me to give you." Solomon answered,

"You have shown great kindness to your servant, my father David, because he was faithful to you and righteous and upright in heart. You have continued this great kindness to him and have given him a son to sit on his throne this very day. "Now, LORD my God, you have made your servant king in place of my father David. But I am only a little child and do not know how to carry out my duties. Your servant is here among the people you have chosen, a great people, too numerous to count or number. So give your servant a discerning heart to govern your people and to distinguish between right and wrong. For who is able to govern this great people of yours?" The Lord was pleased that Solomon had asked for this. So God said to him, "Since you have asked for this and not for long life or wealth for yourself, nor have asked for the death of your enemies but for discernment in administering justice, I will do what you have asked. I will give you a wise and discerning heart, so that there will never have been anyone like you, nor will there ever be.

JUST SPEAK LIFE

If you had a tape recorder on you recording your every word for the entire day, would you be surprised at what you hear when you listen to it? Do you allow all kind of stuff come out of your mouth on a daily basis not realizing the effect that this can have? The Bible declares that life and death are in the power of the tongue. This means that you have the power to speak a word and bring it to life. What an awesome power to have. You just have to know how to use it. If you have a few struggles with your finances, instead of saying you are broke, say that you are blessed. If you feel sick, command your body to line up with the word of God then decree and declare that you are heal, whole and complete in Jesus Christ. Change your vocabulary. Speak over yourself. Just because a situation may seem a certain way, you do not have to repeat what you see. You bring change about in that situation by speaking into the atmosphere.

Have you ever had negative words spoken over you? Maybe you did not say the words yourself, but someone else said it about you. I encourage you to cancel those negative words spoken over you as well. If someone tells you that you are not special, you are dumb, you will never be anything in life, do not receive it. Make a declaration over yourself of the very opposite of what they have said. Decree and declare into the atmosphere that not only are you special, but you are one of a kind. Think for just a moment about a particular situation where someone said something negative about you and how it made you feel. Now think about a situation when someone said something positive about you and how it made you feel. Analyzing these two scenarios should help you understand the power that lies in the words that proceed out of one's mouth.

> The Bible declares that life and death are in the power of the tongue. This means that you have the power to speak a word and bring it to life. What an awesome power to have.

For those who have children, it is essential you understand the power your words have with your children. You already know they mimic and copy everything you do, but they also copy what you say. If you do a lot of fussing and cussing around them, there is no need to wonder why they turn around and behave the same way. Not only that, but it is important that while we speak over ourselves, we must speak life over them as well. Speak greatness into them. Tell them that they are special, they are unique, and that they're beautiful. Do not ever talk down to your children or discourage them.

My oldest daughter loves princesses. I remember once she was talking about princesses, she told me she was one of them. I politely corrected her. I told her she was not Princess Ariel, Snow White or any other princess she saw on the cartoon, she was Princess Triniti. I told her that she is her own unique princess and that she does not have to be like all the other ones she sees on TV. I use this example because I want my children to have their own identity. I want them to be proud about who they are. Therefore, I constantly make it a point to speak a life of uniqueness and individuality into them. If there is something they say that's not positive, I will come behind them and change it. Especially with my girls being so young, it is important for me that they know who they are and whose they are before they have to get out there and experience the cruel and evil ways of this world.

Praying verbally is also important because there is power that comes behind declaring your prayers out loud. You are releasing your words into the atmosphere. Doing so is a wonderful tool to overcome the wiles of the devil. The main way he will try to attack is through your mind and if you can't get your mind right, how can you focus on God while praying silently in your head? You can't because your mind will go in so many different directions with distractions. If you pray out loud, you are more inclined to focus on what you are saying and not the other distractions around you.

You can pray to God by having a normal conversation with Him like you would anyone else. Also, when you pray use your Bible. God says that we are to put Him in remembrance of His word. Read scripture out loud. Decree and declare them over yourself. I know a lot of times when I read scripture I put my name in there. I make it personal. You can too. In addition, using books is a great way to pray out loud. When you have prayer books, they are already sectioned off in different topics and formatted, so all you have to do is read it. Does it make it less effective because you did not write it? Absolutely not. The way I look at it is it's no different than asking someone else to pray for you. Your focus needs to be on using the power that God has given and getting those words into the atmosphere.

Words can build up and they can also tear down. God chose to reveal Himself to man through words, the Holy Bible. A lot of the impact you have on others comes through the words you speak out of our mouth. I am a firm believer that what you say is also a direct reflection of what is in your heart. As the Bible says in Luke chapter 6, out of the abundance of the heart the mouth speaks. So my questions to you, what are you saying to others? What are you saying to yourself? About yourself? Use the power that God has given you. Just speak life.

Life Tools:

Proverbs 18:21 KJV "Death and life are in the power of the tongue: and they that love it shall eat the fruit thereof."

Proverbs 16:24 NIV "Gracious words are a honeycomb, sweet to the soul and healing to the bones." Matthew 12:37 ESV "For by your words you will be justified, and by your words you will be condemned."

Job 22:28 KJV "Thou shalt also decree a thing, and it shall be established unto thee: and the light shall shine upon thy ways."

MAKE THE MOST OF IT

Lately, I've been thinking about how the environment you are in can affect your state of mind. I was thinking of this because I was reminiscing on how it was when I first moved overseas. Coming from the United States, the move literally flipped my world upside down. I absolutely despised it at first. My mind set was already in a negative place in the beginning because I had never been so far away from my family. When we got here the weather was cold, there was snow everywhere, our home is in a small country area where there really isn't much around, it is cold, I did not like the food, I did not understand the language and did I mention it was very, very cold. It took me about a year to really adapt and accept the fact that I was living in a foreign land. In that year of adjustment I was not a very happy camper. I did not want to go anywhere. I did meet a few nice people but within a few months they all slowly started moving back to the states. It was just a very tough transition for me.

I said all of that to say this, I was in a new environment and even though I did not like it, I allowed it to control me in a sense that it changed my entire outlook on life. I allowed it to stop me and slow me down from truly operating in the full purpose of me being here. I knew that God had sent me over here for a reason, and oddly enough I even had a strong spirit of expectation coming over. I was expecting great things, but I was so stuck on me and being selfish that God could not begin to work in me like He wanted to. Instead of me making the most of this new country I was living in, I chose to be miserable. That's right, I made a decision. Therefore I was unable to be very effective because I was so stuck in my unhappy living situation.

How do you still fulfill your purpose and make the most out of situations where you are unhappy? This is a tough question to answer. I think it all goes back to perspective and not allowing your environment, or even people you surround yourself with to hold you back. You have to accept life as it is handed to you. You must decide to make the most of any situation. Do not get caught up in the who, what, when, where or why.

Often times people complain about the environment at their place of employment and how it has a negative impact on them. I can see this happening, mainly because your workplace is somewhere you typically go on a regular basis. This is no different than when children go to school and their behavior begins to rub off on each other. For Christians however, having your own, individual, personal relationship with God is how this can be avoided. When you have your own special relationship with Him, you realize more and more about who He is. You also realize more and more who you are in Him. When you know who you are in Christ, you have a confidence about yourself. You go places knowing you have the power and authority to shift the atmosphere. Whether it is work, school, or the grocery store; wherever you go you take God with you. Instead

Whether it is to work, school, or the grocery store; wherever you go you take God with you. Instead of the folks around you having a negative impact on you, why don't you begin to have a positive impact on them? You shift the atmosphere and watch as the roles are reversed.

of the folks around you having a negative impact on you, why don't you begin to have a positive impact on them? You shift the atmosphere and watch as the roles are reversed.

Learning how to take the good, the bad and the ugly and truly optimize the moment is the purpose of this message. In order for you to fully be used at your utmost potential by God, you have to make a choice to do so. When you make the choice, you should not allow anything, including your environment to stop you from moving forward and walking in your destiny.

Life Tools:

Romans 12:2 ESV "Do not be conformed to this world, but be transformed by the renewal of your mind, that by testing you may discern what is the will of God, what is good and acceptable and perfect."

Philippians 2:5 KJV "Let this mind be in you, which was also in Christ Jesus:"

BLESSED TO BE A BLESSING

Have you ever stopped to think about just how blessed you truly are? When I do, I just get so overjoyed because I know that God does not have to do anything for me. Lord knows I truly do not deserve it but He does it because He loves me. The unmerited love that He shows to His people is simply amazing. The same way that God loves you, you should love others and bless them. God wants you to reciprocate the love He shows to you. The way you do this is by of course loving Him. There really isn't anything tangible you can give to God. You would never be able to even half way compare to God's giving. He wants you to reciprocate His giving by giving yourself to Him and by giving to other people.

When I say blessing, I am not only talking about tangible things such as money. A blessing can also be your time, a listening ear, a phone call, a kind word, a text message, an email, a hug or even a smile. All of these are ways in which you can bless other people. I know it always blesses me when I am in a store or anywhere really and the person walking past smiles. A simple smile never hurt anyone.

Random acts of kindness. What an awesome way to not only make someone's day, but to truly show them the love of God. Have you ever paid for the person's food behind you at the drive thru? Purchased the person in line next to you at the grocery store's groceries? Paid for gas for a stranger at the gas pump next to you who happened to be there at the same time you were? These are all random acts of kindness and I would love to see more of it. I'm sure God would too. After all, kindness is contagious and that's something we could really stand to see spread around the world now and days.

My point is this, invest in someone. We invest in businesses; stocks, bonds and everything else so why not invest in people. Other things are material and can be easily replaced, but souls are eternal. Your kind word or deed may be the seed that God uses to bring someone to Christ. God is working in and through us every day all day.

Remember, to whom much is given, much is required. God has entrusted you with much with an expectation that you bless others the same way.

Therefore, your aim should be to bless others by sharing the resources and knowledge that you have with whomever is in need. I challenge you all to make an effort and go out of your way to bless someone else today. Matter fact, I'll be even more specific not just someone else but a complete stranger. Spread the love and I guarantee as you give to others, it will be given back to you in good measure, pressed down and shaken together.

Life Tools:

Hebrews 13:16 NIV "And do not forget to do good and to share with others, for with such sacrifices God is pleased."

Genesis 12:2 NLT "I will make you into a great nation. I will bless you and make you famous, and you will be a blessing to others."

DON'T WORRY BE HAPPY

"And who of you by being worried can add a single hour to your life?" (Matthew 6:27 NASB). Life is full of uncertainties and will be until the day we leave this earth. The issue is that it seems to be human nature for people to constantly worry. To stop from worrying all the time, I feel as though you have to learn how to bring your mind, body and spirit under subjection. If a problem can be solved, why worry about it? And vice versa, if a problem cannot be solved why worry about it? It's simply a matter of putting things into the right viewpoint.

I can say that a lot of times when an issue presents itself in my life, the first thing I tend to do is try to figure out a solution. I make it a point not to spend too much time focusing on the problem itself, although there have been some times when I have allowed my emotions to get the best of me. Hindsight is 20/20 and I can honestly say in those times when I let my emotions get the best of me, besides feeling horrible on the inside I lost a wonderful gift that God gave, time. Time where I could have been happy, time I could have had joy, time I could have been at peace. I've said before how precious time is and of course you know once it is gone you can never get it back. In addition, think about all the other irrational things your emotions can make you do. All for what? A situation that nine times out of ten you have no control over anyway. Or the control that you do have will not solve anything by wrecking your nerves over it.

Here's something I want you to do, think about an issue you were worrying about a year ago today. If you can even remember something from that long ago, you can also see how that same situation has now been turned around. It is tough to see it while you're going through, but as the saying goes, there is always light at the end of the tunnel. I encourage you to focus on that light.

Do not worry about anything. Instead you must pray about everything. As you focus on the light at the end of the tunnel, trust God. Give your burdens to the Lord and He will take care of you. Walk in the joy, happiness, love and peace that God gives. Find comfort and peace through Scripture that promises you hope and a future. Gain knowledge on how to live free from worry by meditating on the Word and casting your cares upon Jesus.

Life Tools:

Matthew 11:28-30 NLT " Then Jesus said, "Come to me, all of you who are weary and carry heavy burdens, and I will give you rest. Take my yoke upon you. Let me teach you, because I am humble and gentle at heart, and you will find rest for your souls. For my yoke is easy to bear, and the burden I give you is light."

1 Peter 5:6-7 KJV " Humble yourselves therefore under the mighty hand of God, that He may exalt you in due time: Casting all your care upon him; for He careth for you."

TWO SIMPLE LETTERS...N-O!

Learning how to say no is one of the most difficult but most powerful lessons a person can learn in life. It's funny because on the flip side, hearing no can also be one of the most difficult but most powerful things to hear. This goes for children and adults. Most people just have a tendency to want what you want, when you want it. As a parent, what I would call that is being spoiled. The desire to have is not always bad, but you have to know that everything you want is not necessary what you need.

God taught me this about a year after I graduated from college with my undergraduate degree. I got a job that I thought I had always wanted and ended up being extremely miserable. He gave me what I wanted to show me that it was not what I needed. If you would learn this concept, then I think it will be easier to receive it when someone tells you no. On many occasions, I have prayed and made my petition known to God and not gotten what I asked for. I am sure you can relate. I would actually get mad sometimes because I did not understand why He was telling me no. I later came to realize that most of the time what appeared to be a no, was more of a not right now or I have something better for you. My inability to see beyond my present situation caused me to want something that appeared good, when God had great waiting for me around the corner. Stop letting two simple letters make you feel like it is the end of the world. Whether you hear no from God or from man, take it in stride and keep it moving.

Learning how to say no is one of the most difficult, yet most powerful lessons a person can learn in life.

Why is it that people also have a tendency to shy away from telling people no? Yes, we should help others. Yes, we should bless them. And yes, there are some times when you will have to be willing to just say no. It's as simple as that. Sometimes your no is what people need to hear because they have been told yes their whole entire life. Saying no is a way to bring them back to reality.

Not to mention the fact that saying no gives your 'yes' that much more power. If you say yes all the time, how powerful is it really? Doing so could even cause you to be taken for granted. So let's make it personal, why are you so afraid to tell folks no? Is it because you are afraid to hurt their feelings or disappoint them? Is it because you want to please people? Is it because you feel as though they will reject you? Are you afraid of what the response will be? I'm sure there are several reasons. Nevertheless, I've learned that when you say yes to everyone all the time, there are instances when you could possibly be rejecting yourself. It is ok to bless others as I've mentioned before. Selfless service is always great. On the other hand, what's not so great is doing so much for others that you completely forget about yourself. If something happens to you, then what?

Here's what I want you to do. Ask God to increase your spirit of discernment as well as to open your spiritual ears so that when you are pulled on by others you will know which direction you should be going in. Never allow your kindness to be mistaken for a weakness. If you allow your emotions to get the best of you, at times you could possibly end up in situations that you were never meant to be in. If you are truly in tune with the spirit and the voice of God and your discernment is heightened you will know how to not only react but respond to people accordingly. All in all, if you think about it, two simple letters N-O can truly be empowering. I am not saying tell everybody no from now on. I am saying make your yes powerful. When you say yes to others also make sure you are not saying no to yourself. More importantly, make sure you are listening to the voice of your Father and being led by His spirit and not your emotions. It is ok to just say NO.

Life Tools:

Ephesians 5:15-16 NLT "So be careful how you live. Don't live like fools, but like those who are wise. Make the most of every opportunity in these evil days.

Proverbs 16:3 NIV "Commit to the LORD whatever you do, and he will establish your plans."

Matthew 6:33 KJV "But seek ye first the kingdom of God, and his righteousness; and all these things shall be added unto you."

LET'S GO BACK TO THE BASICS

We are now in the new millennium and things have changed so much over the past two decades. Technology has most certainly advanced and the way you go about your everyday life has just been transformed all together. Right now for a brief moment, I want to go back to the basics. Not knocking technology because I think it is great to advance and move forward. Certain things however, seem to have gotten away from us. I can remember as a child not having to worry about issues such as obesity. We played outside literally all day long. Our parents would have to make us come inside in the evening time. Now, children, teenagers and even adults are on the computer all the time or playing video games. They have no concept of what it means to go out and play. Another issue I've noticed and seems to be getting even worse is a matter of respect. There was a time in my life where I could never imagine anyone asking for something and not saying please or thank you, or doing something wrong and not apologizing.

Unfortunately, that is not the case in today's society. People just seem have some type of sense of entitlement and feel as though the world owes them something. It is sad because first of all, that is not true. No one owes you anything. Secondly, whatever happened to the golden rule? You treat others as you would want to be treated. Always consider how you would feel if another person acted the way you act. Would you be happy with their behavior or would it make you angry. If it makes you angry then that means if you do it, it will make someone else angry and you do not need to do it.

As an adult, you should be a role model. Not only teaching those younger than you proper conduct through your words, but by exemplifying proper conduct in your actions. It is a known fact that children will mimic what they see whether the actions are good or bad. As an adult, you should not allow the actions of other people to cause you to distort the example that you set. What I mean is, if someone else is being rude or mean instead of copying their behavior you set the example and behave in a manner that is more becoming.

Manners are in your heart. Interpersonal skills such as being polite, listening, apologizing when you are wrong, saying please, thank you, you're welcome, and sharing with others reveal the good manners in your heart. Manners cost nothing and are priceless. True indeed, we all have super busy lives, but there is always time for courtesy. Be polite, say hello, offer help, smile, and pay a compliment. Use please and thank you. You have to get back to the basics, so you can be the example that Jesus Christ wants you to be.

Life Tools:

Luke 6:31 NIV "Do to others as you would have them do to you"

Galatians 5:22-23 NLT "But the Holy Spirit produces this kind of fruit in our lives: love, joy, peace, patience, kindness, goodness, faithfulness, gentleness, and self-control. There is no law against these things!"

HUMILITY

What does it mean to be humble? This is a word I have read a lot about, mostly in the Bible and I have come to learn that humility is not something that comes natural. It is something you should desire, just like wisdom but not something you are expected to know on your own. The reason I say this is because people have been taught differently in modern day society. Women are taught to be independent and know how to take care of themselves. Men are taught to be macho and the breadwinner. Having or showing a modest or low estimate of one's own importance is a direct contradiction to what has just been described. Or is it?

Do you believe it is possible to be humble, yet still take care of business at the same time? People who aren't humble are prideful. Pride is another form of insecurity. It's a mask people tend to hide behind when they can't handle their reality or as I like to call it, the truth. They are constantly talking about themselves, bragging and often considered to be conceited and stuck-up. I've known a few people like this in my day and in spite of all they have accomplished, if anything, their personality seems to make me think very little of them. I am a person who feels like your deeds and actions should speak for themselves. You should not think it is necessary to tell people your list of accomplishments when they first meet you. I applaud hard work and strongly believe that it will be rewarded in the end, but let your reward speak for you. Once you talk about it all the time and feel the need to tell everyone, I begin to question your motive behind it all in the first place. Were you only doing it so you would have something to boast about? If that's the case, all of what you are talking about will be very short lived.

> People who aren't humble are prideful. Pride is another form of insecurity. It's a mask people tend to hide behind when they can't handle their reality or as I like to call it, the truth.

To be humble is something that requires effort. You have to make a decision to not get the "big head". Decide that you will work hard, you will succeed, but you will never forget where you came from. I always say no matter what new endeavor you pursue, never despise small beginnings. If you start small, it will be a constant reminder of where you came from and how far you have come. Not only that, it will also show you just how far you can still go. When you are humble, you have an innate ability to always strive for greatness, which leads me to believe that continued success is inevitable.

The true and undying power of mankind, that's you and me, is found in submission. Submission to whom you might ask? Submission to God. No matter what your social status, pay grade, or job title you must always be willing to submit yourself to the will of God for your life. You should wake up every morning asking God what His will is for you. Many times we tell God what we want to do and that is backwards. Before Jesus went to the cross, He prayed and said not my will God but Your will be done. He humbled Himself to the will of the Father for us. In His short 33 years of walking this earth Jesus was the ultimate example of what it means to be humble. Allow our Lord and Savior to be your guide as you live a life of humility. Please do not misunderstand what I am saying. I truly, truly, truly believe that hard work deserves acknowledgement but don't do it for the acknowledgement. Examine your motives. Humility is not thinking less of yourself, but thinking of yourself less. It is a character trait required in order to be truly effective in life.

Life Tools:

Proverbs 11:2 NIV "When pride comes, then comes disgrace, but with humility comes wisdom."

Luke 14:11 NLT "For those who exalt themselves will be humbled, and those who humble themselves will be exalted."

James 4:10 NLT "Humble yourselves before the Lord, and he will lift you up in honor."

KNOW YOUR WORTH

Do you know just how precious you are? Do you know how valuable you are? If you had to give a dollar amount to how much you are worth, could you do it? I started off asking these questions because so many people do not know the answer. Why is that? If you don't know your own worth and value, then don't expect someone else to calculate it for you. I am here to tell you that you should always know your worth. The key to truly living life to the fullest is coming into the knowledge of understanding how valuable you are. Not your house, your car or your jewelry, but YOU.

Think for a moment about this, if you were a prince or princess (such as Prince Harry or his mom Princess Diana). How would the way you live your life be different?

The key to truly living life to the fullest is coming into the knowledge of understanding how valuable you are. Not your house, your car or your jewelry, but YOU.

You would probably walk around with your head a little bit higher. You would have a bit more self-confidence. And I'm sure there are certain things you wouldn't stand for or allow to happen to you or around you.

Now, what if I told you that you are royalty? As a child of the most High God, you are a royal priesthood because your Heavenly Father is the King of Kings. Your worth comes from God, so to answer the questions I started off with would mean that you are priceless. That's right, priceless. There is no amount of money or tangible things that could ever be sufficient to describe your value. And to top that off, no matter what has happened in your past or present and whatever happens in your future, you will never lose your value. Isn't that amazing? God is not like man that He should lie, so if He said it in His word than that settles it. No going back. Now that you have this piece of inside information, I want you to act like it.

Surround yourself with people who know your worth. I remember something my pastor once said that was a true revelation for me. We should be around people who are concerned with our soul. When I heard this, a light bulb just went off in my head. If the people who are around you are not concerned about you mind, body and spirit then you don't want to be connected to them. Sometimes it can be hard to tell who these people are. Pray and ask God to help you discern who is for you all the way around. He will reveal those individuals. As He does, you will learn to appreciate enjoy being around folks who are real and who can appreciate you for exactly who you are and vice versa.

Please let this serve as a reminder. A lot of times we say we know our worth and "act" strong, and then as soon as the enemy sends someone to tear us down we allow them to do just that. When you know your worth, no one can come along to make you feel worthless. Remember, your value does not decrease based on someone else's inability to see your worth. Your worth is determined by God. He has the final say and He has already declared in His word who you are to Him. That's really all that matters.

Life Tools:

1 Peter 2:9 KJV "But ye are a chosen generation, a royal priesthood, an holy nation, a peculiar people; that ye should shew forth the praises of him who hath called you out of darkness into his marvelous light:"

Deuteronomy 28:13 KJV "And the LORD shall make thee the head, and not the tail; and thou shalt be above only, and thou shalt not be beneath; if that thou hearken unto the commandments of the LORD thy God, which I command thee this day, to observe and to do them:"

Numbers 23:19 NLT "God is not a man, so he does not lie. He is not human, so he does not change his mind. Has he ever spoken and failed to act? Has he ever promised and not carried it through?"

BETTER DAYS AHEAD

Now is the time I want to speak words of encouragement to you. Life can bring many circumstances that make you feel as though you literally have the weight of the world on your shoulders. Other times you feel as though you are so happy you could just burst with joy. I don't know where you are or what you are going through right now (good or bad), but I am here to tell you that better days are ahead. You will not always be in this same place.

Just like this beautiful earth that God created, we all go through different seasons in life. The good news is, seasons change. Some stick around a little longer than others, but eventually they do change. Growing up in Florida, everyone used to say we only get one season the entire year. Yes, it is hot in Florida but we get more than one season throughout the year. The summer season just lasts a lot longer. Such is life. One thing I will say is that no matter what season of life you are in, it is important to not become so consumed in the burdens or the blessings that the spotlight is more on them and not on HIM. Better days are ahead, but you must keep the right perspective and not allow anything to become more important than God.

Good, bad or indifferent, the season you are in now is ordained by God. Talk to Him and see what it is He wants you to get out of it. Ask Him what His will is for you at this particular time in life? What is His plan for you at this moment in time? You cannot move forward with the next chapter in your life, the next season of your life if you keep re-reading the last one. God has something better in store waiting for you around the corner; you just need to get in line to receive it. If you are in a good season of your life, it is still time to move forward. Just because something good ends, does not mean that something better won't begin. So my brothers and sisters in Christ be encouraged. Nothing lasts forever. Live each day as if it were your last. Put

A thought provoking concept you should always be mindful of is that your present situation is not your final destination; the best is yet to come.

yourself to the side. Trust God like never before, lean and depend on Him at all times. A thought provoking concept you should always be mindful of is that your present situation is not your final destination; the best is yet to come. I am certain that no matter where you may be in life, some of the best days of your life have not even happened yet. Isn't that such an amazing feeling? So smile and know better days are ahead.

Life Tools:

Jeremiah 29:11 NLT "For I know the plans I have for you," says the LORD. "They are plans for good and not for disaster, to give you a future and a hope."

Galatians 6:9 KJV "And let us not be weary in well doing: for in due season we shall reap, if we faint not."

THE IMPORTANCE OF RIGHT RELATIONSHIPS

A lot of the times when you think about relationships, you think about a romantic relationship. It is not until you consider the definition of what a relationship is that you are truly able to understand that in spite of your marital status, most people are involved in several relationships in their lifetime. For instance, if you have people you consider to be friends then you have relationships with them because you are connected to them. Truth be told, you have a relationship with your employer, the phone company and the cable company, just to name a few. The point is, as long as you are connected, a relationship will always exist. I am not going to talk about having a relationship with the phone company, although it is important to stay on the up and up with them. You and I both know that if you don't, then you probably won't have a phone (Smile). What I would like to talk about however is the importance of right relationships.

Some people are very outgoing and others, such as myself, tend to be a little more of an introvert.

Whatever personality type you have, everyone desires to have friends. People who would make your life different if they did not exist. People, who know you, but choose to love you anyway. Individuals who are there for you no matter what and who you can trust and depend on. Those are concepts that define what I consider to be a true friend. This is also what I think of in regards to what it means to be in a right relationship.

Now all of these things sound good in theory, but my questions is this, how do you know when a person you are in a relationship with is truly a friend? You meet new people everyday and obviously some you connect with better than others. To answer the question however, I'd say that you really do not know. You just have to take a chance. It is tough as a parent however, because in most cases when you are friends with someone your family meets that person, which means now more people are connected and have that relationship.

The dangerous part is when you take that chance only to find out that person was never really a friend in the first place. Stuff happens, I get that and although it hurts, you are able to move on with your life. The most unfortunate part however is that now your children, who are completely innocent, have formed a bond with them and you have to explain to them why that person is no longer apart of your family's life. This has been a real wake up call for me and I want each and every one of you to learn from my mistake.

Please allow me to change my answer a bit from before. I still think you have to take a chance when you meet people, but you are to acknowledge God in all things. This includes whom you should and should not be connected to. I have prayed and asked God to remove people who were not for me and my family and when He actually did, it hurt at first but then I began to thank Him. When you pray to God, be willing to listen and obey His answer. When He answers your prayer, thank Him. Do not get so caught up in temporary contentment that you are not willing to hear or obey what God has to say. Hearing God and obeying Him will prevent you from a whole lot of heartache.

I will be the first to say it is tough to find not just people who are trying to live right, but in my case married people. My husband and I have wanted to connect with other couples who are headed in the same direction we are, both spiritually and mentally. We have come to the realization that we must relinquish our desire to the will of our Father and trust His timing. Often times we get so caught up in what we want, then get excited when we think it has come. Never fully allowing God to show us who's who and what's what. Instead of getting excited, we have to keep a sound mind.

Satan will always send you a 'knock off' or fake version of whatever it is you are asking God for to distract you from the real thing. He knows that when God answers prayer, it is going to draw you even closer in your relationship to Him. The enemy knows that as your relationship with God strengthens it is going to push him further back into hell, where he belongs.

Satan will always send you a 'knock off' or fake version of whatever it is you are asking God for to distract you from the real thing.

In spite of the hardships of life and understanding the ins and outs of relationships, there is good news. I am a friend of God, and so are you.

He is the best friend you could ever have. You never have to worry about Him walking away from you, turning His back on you or hurting you in any way. No greater love than to lay down your life for a friend. That's exactly what our Lord and Savior Jesus Christ did. Please be mindful of your relationships. Pray and ask God who is supposed to be in your life, when they are supposed to be in your life and for how long. That's the answer, simply put. Take a chance, but above all seek God.

Life Tools:

James 2:23 ESV "and the Scripture was fulfilled that says, "Abraham believed God, and it was counted to him as righteousness" – and he was called a friend of God."

John 15:13-15 KJV "Greater love has no man than this, that a man lay down his life for his friends. You are my friends, if you do whatever I command you. From now on I call you not servants; for the servant knows not what his lord does: but I have called you friends; for all things that I have heard of my Father I have made known to you."

SPRINKLED WITH A LITTLE BIT OF 'FAVOR'

The favor of God is such a beautiful thing. There is a common misconception however, when individuals talk about God's favor. People tend to think that everyone gets the same measure of favor and this is not true, hence the phrase "favor ain't fair". There is a difference between just and fair. God is a just God. The Bible declares that He will supply all of your needs, not necessarily all of your wants. Your needs consist of anything you need in life to keep living. Air to breathe, food and water are examples of needs.

God grants favor, but everybody's favor is not going to be equivalent. My favor is not going to be the same as yours, which is not going to be the same for the next person and so on. A great example of this can be found when reading the story in the Bible about the three servants

God grants favor, but everybody's favor is not going to be equivalent. My favor is not going to be the same as yours, which is not going to be the same for the next person and so on.

in Matthew 25. The master gave each of the servants a different amount of bags of silver. He gave one servant five bags, another two bags, and the last servant he gave one bag of silver. Why did he give each one a different amount? He gave each one the amount that he thought they could handle. God does the same thing. He gives us a measure of favor according to not only what we can handle, but where we are spiritually and our relationship with Him.

In the end of this story truly explains it all. When the master came back, the servant whom he entrusted the five bags to now had ten bags, the one he gave two bags now had four and the servant with one bag still ended up with one bag. The first two had enough sense to work with what they had to make more, when the last one simply dug a hole in the ground and left it there. He did not even try to add to it. You have to know what to do with what you have. Often times, you look for the blessing but when you get the blessing you are not a good steward over it. Take care of the little bit that you do have in the very best way possible, and God will add to it. As God has said in His word, when you are faithful over a few things, He will make you a ruler over many.

Just because you have the favor of God on your life does not mean you are going to escape going through your "go-throughs". You are not exempt from difficulty. It does not mean that God does not love you. He is right there with you. Whatever the hard time is you are dealing with God will walk you through, but through it you must go. That is the key, go. You cannot stand still and allow your present situation to stop you from reaching your future.

Favor is goodwill. It is a gift that God gives to those who love Him. Favor is not the blessing itself. It is what releases the blessings. When you have favor on your life, people will do things for you and not even know why they are doing it. Doors will be opened that have never been opened and doors will be closed that can never be opened. This is how favor releases the blessing. There are many examples in the Bible where God's favor upon His people causes them to experience supernatural breakthroughs. Simply put, favor is God's loving kindness.

You will know when you begin to walk in the favor and blessing of the Lord and so will others. Generally people will criticize the favor of God on your life because they cannot claim the rights to your success. I don't know why people have to feel like they have their hand in everything. There are something's you just cannot do. God makes it that way so He can get the glory. Folks who are like this, I call them haters. Instead of them congratulating what God is doing, they get mad and often times jealous. If you have a lot of haters and don't understand why, this could be your reason. These types of people can hurt your feelings if you let them, especially when all you are trying to do is live right. I'm here right now to encourage you to recognize these individuals for who they are and keep on doing your thang. Do not allow their negativity and unhappiness with themselves to cause you to miss what God is doing in your life.

Make this declaration over your life right now, "I am blessed and highly favored of God. I am the head and not the tail. I am above only and not beneath. No weapon formed against me shall prosper because God is for me and He is more than the whole world against me." As you make this declaration, get it down into your spirit. Speak over yourself, encourage yourself and watch God turn around and sprinkle it with a little favor.

Life Tools:

Psalms 90:17 ESV "Let the favor of the Lord our God be upon us, and establish the work of our hands upon us; yes, establish the work of our hands!"

Matthew 25:14-30 NLT "Again, the Kingdom of Heaven can be illustrated by the story of a man going on a long trip. He called together his servants and entrusted his money to them while he was gone. He gave five bags of silver to one, two bags of silver to another, and one bag of silver to the last – dividing it in proportion to their abilities. He then left on his trip. "The servant who received the five bags of silver began to invest the money and earned five more. The servant with two bags of silver also went to work and earned two more. But the servant who received the one bag of silver dug a hole in the ground and hid the master's money. "After a long time their master returned from his trip and called them to give an account of how they had used his money. The servant to whom he had entrusted the five bags of silver came forward with five more and said, 'Master, you gave me five bags of silver to invest, and I have earned five more.' "The master was full of praise. 'Well done, my good and faithful servant. You have been faithful in handling this small amount, so now I will give you many more responsibilities. Let's celebrate together!' "The servant who had received the two bags of silver came forward and said, 'Master, you gave me two bags of silver to invest, and I have earned two more.' "The master said, 'Well done, my good and faithful servant. You have been faithful in handling this small amount, so now I will give you many more responsibilities. Let's celebrate together!' "Then the servant with the one bag of silver came and said, 'Master, I knew you were a harsh man, harvesting crops you didn't plant and gathering crops you didn't cultivate. I was afraid I would lose your money, so I hid it in the earth. Look, here is your money back.' "But the master replied, 'You wicked and lazy servant! If you knew I harvested crops I didn't plant and gathered crops I didn't cultivate, why didn't you deposit my money in the bank? At least I could have gotten some interest on it.' "Then he ordered, 'Take the money from this servant, and give it to the one with the ten bags of silver. To those who use well what they are given, even more will be given, and they will have an abundance. But from those who do nothing, even what little they have will be taken away. Now throw this useless servant into outer darkness, where there will be weeping and gnashing of teeth.'

BE PREPARED

One of the biggest lessons I was taught while growing up was always be prepared. At the time and even to this very day, I understand the importance of preparation. Some people tend to think that preparation takes away from having faith in God. I disagree. I feel as though preparation and faith go hand in hand. You have the faith that God is going to protect you when you get in your car and drive, yet you still put on your seat belt. Or you know that God will provide all of you and your family's needs, yet you still have life insurance. The attitude in which you operate while getting prepared is where faith comes in. If you do something because you do not know if God will do His part or "just in case" God does not do what you think He should, then you are not operating in faith at all. You are leaning and trusting on your own free will more than that of the Father.

You are to most certainly walk by faith, but God gives us common sense as well. Unfortunately, common sense is a flower that does not grow in everyone's garden. Think for a moment, God promised to provide for all creation, even the birds. He does not build a nest for them; He created trees so they can make their own nest. Before they can do that, they have to prepare by gathering sticks and shrubs then knitting them together to make their home.

Preparation is essential in so many different areas of life. God gave us a brain, we have to be smart and use it. A lot of what I was told to do in my younger years, whether it was homework for school, chores around the house, and even work on my actual job; all prepared me for my future. The things you do today help pave the way for tomorrow. As an adult you have to be mindful that not only does it pave the way for tomorrow, it paves the way for the legacy you plan to leave behind for your bloodline. Your children's, children's, children. If you do not have any children, your nieces, nephews and even cousins. You have to think beyond yourself and help pave the way for future generations to come. Think about it like this, blessings happen when preparation meets opportunity. Next time that big opportunity presents itself, if you are prepared, great things can happen.

It is so imperative that you not waste away time because, tomorrow is not promised. There has to be balance in your lifestyle. God gave you the need, need for food, need for water, need for shelter, these types of things. I believe He did so in order to turn you away from everything in the world and focus on Him. By focusing on Him you exercise your faith, and trust that God will do what He says He will do. While also doing your part to make sure you have what you need. You do your part by getting ready. Go to work so you can have income, when the bills come in you are now ready to pay them. Let God do the super and you do the natural.

Jesus is coming back again, so set aside all the preparation of day-to-day life; will your soul be ready? Are you saved? Have you accepted Jesus as your Lord and Savior? Stop saying you aren't ready yet. Ready for what? To be delivered? To be set free? To have peace, love and joy in your heart? God is not expecting you to change anything about your life on your own. All He wants is for you to say yes to Him. If you confess with your mouth, "Jesus is Lord," and believe in your heart that God raised him from the dead, you will be saved. When you do that and begin to build your relationship with Him, He will do the rest. Heaven is real and so is hell. There is no better time than now to prepare for the returning of our Lord and give your life to Christ. No better time than now to get your act together. Stop putting off for tomorrow what you can do today. As the saying goes, 'when you fail to prepare, you prepare to fail'.

Life Tools:

Matthew 24:44 ESV "Therefore you also must be ready, for the Son of Man is coming at an hour you do not expect."

1 Thessalonians 5:2 NLT "For you know quite well that the day of the Lord's return will come unexpectedly, like a thief in the night."

CLEAN UP! CLEAN UP! EVERYBODY DO YOUR SHARE!

One of the most dreadful things on my regular to do list is clean up. I don't know why, it just seems like I could be spending my time doing a whole lot of other stuff. Stuff that's a whole lot more fun. Then of course, when I do get up and start cleaning I am happy that I did because I am able to organize a little more, free up space, get rid of stuff we don't use, and just straighten up. Just like your physical home requires cleaning, so does your spiritual home.

Just like your physical home requires cleaning, so does your spiritual home.

It may be time for you to go on a cleaning spree within yourself. It is time to really do a self-evaluation and get rid of any bondage or strongholds that have been lingering over your life that you may not even realize. Throw away all trash and the junk that is cluttering your life. Divest yourself of anything that is preventing you from operating in your full potential. If you want to be delivered from bondage, strongholds, traps, or any other ploys of the enemy you have to say so. Do not listen to satan and the negative things he has planted in your spirit. Counteract his lies by opening up your mouth and saying, "I will not be oppressed, repressed or depressed. I will not be discouraged." Whatever he is trying to hold you hostage with, you make a declaration of the exact opposite. Tell the devil he is a liar.

When you are cleaning, the first thing you have to do is identify whatever it is you need to throw away. If you don't recognize the junk, whether it's in front of you or hidden behind the couch, it will stay put right where it is. Therefore, once you acknowledge what the enemy is doing and put him on front street, he has no choice but to back off because now you have called him out. Once you put him in his place, this is where true purification and cleansing begins.

If you have other old baggage such as bitterness or the inability to forgive, you have to let that go also. Any form of sin can weigh you down, but bitterness and the inability to forgive are two strongholds that are similar to old boxes in the basement you just can't seem to throw away. You have become so familiar with it sometimes you don't even realize how it is hindering your life. I am talking to myself on this one, because I can honestly say I have overcome a lot during my spiritual journey but this is one area that seems to be a bit more difficult than others to overcome. The beautiful thing about having a relationship with God and hearing from Him is that He never intended for you to make any of these changes on your own. You cannot clean yourself, even if you tried. God has given you an instruction manual to use. It is the top selling book all over the world. It's up to you to open it up and follow the instructions.

When you draw close to God, study your instruction manual which is the word of God, spend time in prayer, fast and do all you can to be near Him your body and heart will go through a spiritual makeover. As the relationship develops there are positive consequences that come along with it. Your mind begins to change, the way you talk begins to change, and even the way you think begins to change. So, as you clean up your spirit man, be excited for the change that is bound to come with it. Pardon my language ladies and gentlemen, but aint nobody gone be mad but the devil. Now it's time to clean up, clean up, everybody do your share!

Life Tools:

Psalms 51:10 KJV "Create in me a clean heart, O God; and renew a right spirit within me."

Luke 6:45 NLT "A good person produces good things from the treasury of a good heart, and an evil person produces evil things from the treasury of an evil heart. What you say flows from what is in your heart."

DON'T QUIT!

Although I've never participated in a marathon I always find them to be quite interesting. Most sporting events, people are in it to compete and win. With marathons however, there are hundreds, sometimes even thousands of people that participate. I'm pretty sure that when 95% of the people that sign up for the marathon aren't signing up to win. They are probably participating as a personal goal or maybe they may even want to support someone else. Automatically this lets me know they are in it and plan to finish the race completely. Sounds good at first, but when the actual race begins things may play out a little differently. Some people run it gracefully all the way through. Others have physical ailments that come up and hinder them from completing the race (cramps, dehydration, etc.). I want to talk about those hindrances. You may not be in an actual marathon race right now, but your life certainly feels like one. There are moments that go by effortlessly. All is well, no setbacks just smooth sailing. Then as the season in your life changes, here come those obstacles and stumbling blocks. They come to stop you in your tracks and cause you to give up.

I'm here today to tell you, don't quit. Endurance is essential if you really want to get all that you can out of life. You have to possess the ability deep down inside to keep running. If you can't run, keep walking and if you can't walk get down and crawl. Whatever you do, you have to keep moving. Many times the enemy will send disruption in our life to cause us to stop. Remember that's his job (to kill, steal and destroy). Unfortunately, sometimes his ploys and tactics work because you allow your flesh to take over, instead of allowing your spirit man to rise up on the inside of you. This is why the Bible tells us that we are to kill our flesh daily.

Are you tired of starting over in life? Well, stop quitting. Stop allowing things (people, situations, circumstances) to cause you to lose focus of what God has ahead of you.

Are you tired of starting over in life? Well, stop quitting. Stop allowing things (people, situations, circumstances) to cause you to lose focus of what God has ahead of you. When I talk about endurance I always think about when Moses brought the people of Israel out of Egypt. The place where God was taking them to was between 200–400 miles away. If you do 10 miles a day, which is very possible, they could have been there in 40 days. Some people say it could have been even quicker than that. Instead however, the voyage took 40 years. Here's why. During their journey they decided to murmur, complain, they even stopped walking and what's even worse is they continued to look back on what was and what used to be. Doing so caused them to literally miss what was right in front of them. Stop giving your past so much attention. Leave your past behind you; it is there for a reason. Learn from it and keep it moving.

No matter what is going on around you, make up in your mind that you are going to endure to the very end. You have to get that down in your spirit. Build yourself up, so when the devil tries to tear you down, that's all he can do is try. God has so much in store for you. He loves you more than you love yourself. Hang in there. Don't give up. Don't quit. You got this. How am I so sure of that? Cause God's got you!

Life Tools:

Matthew 24:13 NLT "But the one who endures to the end will be saved."

James 1:2-4 NLT " Dear brothers and sisters, when troubles come your way, consider it an opportunity for great joy. For you know that when your faith is tested, your endurance has a chance to grow. So let it grow, for when your endurance is fully developed, you will be perfect and complete, needing nothing."

Hebrews 12:1 KJV "Wherefore seeing we also are compassed about with so great a cloud of witnesses, let us lay aside every weight, and the sin which doth so easily beset us, and let us run with patience the race that is set before us,"

OPERATE IN EXCELLENCE

Everyone is at a different level in life. It is easy to say that women mature quicker than men, or men work harder than women but in actuality these are all generalizations that may not be true. Some men mature very quickly and there are several women that would outwork a man any day. Nevertheless, you must be mindful of generalizations and not get so caught up in what this person is or is not doing. I feel like individuals in society would be so much farther in life if everyone focused on their own business and not allow yourself to get over-involved in other people's life. In order to move ahead during your existence on this earth, get on your level and stay there. Whatever your level is, work it to the very best of your ability. Do you. Mind your own business. Focus in on where you are and what you are doing. Operating in excellence where you are now will have a direct impact on your future.

As children of God, we are on different levels spiritually. We all have a special level of closeness to God. The closer you are to Him, the more spiritually mature you will be. Know where you are in your relationship with Christ. Know your level. I will say it again, when you know your level operate in excellence on that level. If you know you are an intercessor, do not attempt to pray like other people. Pray whatever God has placed inside of you the best way you know how and do so with excellence. If your service to God is to clean bathrooms or cut the grass at the church, do so with excellence. If you are on the praise and worship team, study the lyrics to the song so you can know the words. Come Sunday morning open up your mouth and sing every week like it is your last.

Know where you are in your relationship with Christ. Know your level. When you know your level, operate in excellence on that level.

When you operate in excellence, you are honoring God. Everything you do, whether it is for the church or on your job or in your home you must do it to the glory of God. I know firsthand how easy it is to get caught up in the people around us. When you have people lifting you and encouraging you that is all good, as long as it is received the right way. On the opposite end of that however, the moment they do or say something to tear you down you are ready to walk away. This is not the appropriate response. You have to put things into perspective. Walking away from any service that you know God has called you to do is not walking away from man. It is really God that you are walking away from. If you keep your focus on Him and not man, you are showing God how much you love Him and how much you are truly committed to serving Him. Don't allow the enemy to cause you to lose focus.

Excellence does not come by mistake. It is a habit. It is something you must make a conscious effort to strive for. You have to do it on a consistent basis, relentlessly striving for more and better until it becomes second nature. As you complete the duties of everyday life, do so with excellence and make your Heavenly Father proud.

Life Tools:

2 Timothy 3:16-17 KJV "All scripture is given by inspiration of God, and is profitable for doctrine, for reproof, for correction, for instruction in righteousness: That the man of God may be perfect, thoroughly furnished to all good works."

Colossians 3:22-24 KJV "servants, obey in all things your masters according to the flesh; not with eye-service, as men pleasers; but in singleness of heart, fearing God; And whatever you do, do it heartily, as to the Lord, and not to men; Knowing that of the Lord you shall receive the reward of the inheritance: for you serve the Lord Christ."

I'M SAVED AND I'M PROUD!

While conducting a little research, I noticed there are a few definitions for the word bold, but the one I want to talk about today is the ability to take risks. When I think of bold, I think of someone who is confident and courageous. That being said, the opposite of bold is to be weak or cowardly. A person who is bold may be willing to risk shame or rejection if it means that they will stand up for what they believe in. I said all of that to say this, one thing I have never quite understood about the Body of Christ is their sense of weakness. I have seen Muslims on the street corner selling newspapers and bean pies, all while proclaiming their faith. Jehovah's Witnesses come around to people's home every day, literally all over the world (thought they only did it in the States until I moved to Europe) telling them what they believe. And I mean they are bold with it too. They will look through windows, ring doorbells, walk in garages, and do whatever it takes to talk to you. I have a childhood friend whose family is Jehovah's Witness. He explained a lot of their beliefs to me and their reasoning for going out and talking to people the way they do. I did not agree with what he said, and we agreed to disagree. To this day however, I cannot help but respect their perseverance and boldness. They are taking a stand for what they believe in and telling as many people as they can about it.

When it comes to the Body of Christ, it seems as though we are afraid to stand up for what we believe in. We press our way to church on Sunday and have an awesome time in the Lord. When we leave the four walls of the church building, if someone talks about Jesus Christ or God we are afraid to make our beliefs known. Why is that? Why is the body of Christ not on the street corners proclaiming the gospel of Jesus to all who will

> It's time for the body of Christ to stand up! Stand for what you believe in. I'm not just talking about abortion rights, sexuality or some of the other big political issues. I am talking every day, normal conversations letting people know that God loves them and teaching them how they can receive salvation.

hear? Why are we not knocking on doors, looking through windows and walking in garages to tell people about salvation? Is it because we are closet Christians? You only want certain people to know what you believe in so you don't hurt anyone's feelings. Or are you afraid to defend your faith? Atheist will tell you in a heartbeat that they don't believe in God. Why not tell others that you do believe in God?

It's time for the body of Christ to stand up! Stand for what you believe in. I'm not just talking about abortion rights, sexuality or some of the other big political issues. I am talking every day, normal conversations letting people know that God loves them and teaching them how they can receive salvation. Take the time to spread the good news about who Jesus is and why He died on the cross. Provide the tools necessary to help others in their walk with God. Overall, we need to be doing the work that Jesus Christ commanded us to do before He ascended back into heaven.

It's time for true believers to be bold in your faith. You have to let the enemy know that he is not the only one who does not mind taking risks. You must show him that you are courageous and confident about the things of the Kingdom of God. Not within yourself, but the Holy Spirit that is within you.

My prayer has been that the spirit of God would rise within me whenever I am in a situation that I may be uncomfortable or a bit anxious to do the work that I know God has called me to do. When I think about Jesus and what He did for me, how He died on Calvary to set me free. When I think about how He turned my life around and showed mercy when I was not even thinking about Him. I want to be bold for Christ. And you should too. I'm sure when you think about the goodness of God; you just cannot keep it to yourself. Don't be a closet believer, only professing your faith one or two days out of the week. Step out of the closet and let the world know that the body of Christ is strong. You need to be committed to being about your Father's Business. Right now more than ever, people need to know what it means to accept Jesus Christ as Lord and Savior. They need to understand the difference between religion and having an actual relationship with God. My brothers and sister in Christ, it's time to get to work! It's time for some Holy Boldness! Say it loud, I'm saved and I'm proud!

Life Tools:

Acts 1:8 NLT "But you will receive power when the Holy Spirit comes upon you. And you will be my witnesses, telling people about me everywhere – in Jerusalem, throughout Judea, in Samaria, and to the ends of the earth."

Deuteronomy 31:6 ESV "Be strong and courageous. Do not fear or be in dread of them, for it is the LORD your God who goes with you. He will not leave you or forsake you."

KEEP SEEKING, KEEP ASKING, KEEP KNOCKING

It is amazing to see my two girls play together. I can remember when they were both just small tiny babies, and now they run around the house playing all the time. What's even funnier to me is that my youngest is so much more persistent. She does not care who, what, when, where or why. When she wants something she is going to do whatever she needs to do to get it. She will climb on a chair, crawl underneath a table, whatever it takes.

What if grown-ups were as persistent as children? What if we did not let anything stop us from living our life on purpose and fulfilling the call that God has for us? What if the body of Christ made up in our mind that no matter what tactics the enemy uses, we are going to do just as the word says; keep seeking, keep asking, and keep knocking?

You have to get to the point where you are consistent and persistent in life. Of course, life brings change but what I mean about being consistent and persistent is more of a state of mind.

To have the right state of mind, or should I say righteous state of mind, you have to read and study the word God persistently. If you have a busy schedule, make time in your day to spend with God. If you have unexpected events take place during your day, still make time. Even if means you get a little less sleep, you do what you have to do because you are persistent.

You have to understand that it is your consistency and persistence that builds your relationship with God. The same way you are persistent on your job, doing a task that should be completed by eight or nine people, yet you do it by yourself. Yeah it may cause you to work longer hours, miss a few breaks, and even work on your day off but nevertheless, you will get the job done. You have to have that same tenacity when it comes to your spiritual walk. Matter of fact, you cannot afford not to.

I will say it again; you have to keep seeking God, keep asking, and keep knocking. The story of the persistent widow in Luke 18 is one that you should pay close attention to. Did the widow know that the judge was going to change his mind? No. She just knew she had a petition to make and she made it. She did not go only one time. She kept going back until finally the judge changed his mind and granted her request. Jesus uses this parable to show that God is our judge and He will bring about justice to His people, just as this judge did to the widow. The beautiful thing about the Bible is that it is a guide for life. Everything that you could possibly think of having to go through is already written in the book. You just have to open it up and read it.

Life Tools:

Luke 18:1-8 NIV "Then Jesus told his disciples a parable to show them that they should always pray and not give up. He said: "In a certain town there was a judge who neither feared God nor cared what people thought. And there was a widow in that town who kept coming to him with the plea, 'Grant me justice against my adversary.' "For some time he refused. But finally he said to himself, 'Even though I don't fear God or care what people think, yet because this widow keeps bothering me, I will see that she gets justice, so that she won't eventually come and attack me!' And the Lord said,

"Listen to what the unjust judge says. And will not God bring about justice for his chosen ones, who cry out to him day and night? Will he keep putting them off? I tell you, he will see that they get justice, and quickly. However, when the Son of Man comes, will he find faith on the earth?"

Romans 2:7 NIV "To those who by persistence in doing good seek glory, honor and immortality, he will give eternal life."

BE IN HEALTH

How well do you take care of your belongings? Most people will say they take pretty good care of their car, home and clothes, etc. When you compare these things, to those that are simply given to us there is a distinct difference. The items you feel as though you work hard for, you tend to value a little more, therefore prompting you to take better care of those things. On the other hand, things which are simply given to you or we don't have to work as hard for you might not take care of them as well.

The Bible declares that you are to be good stewards over the things you have. A lot of times you only think about tangible things. Another aspect of life you have to be a good steward over is your body. A person's body, mind and spiritual nature are all mutually dependent upon one another. It is nearly impossible for one to function at full capacity if the others are not. I am not a big fan of exercise and I think that is mainly because for a good period of my life, a lot of my everyday regular activities involve exercise already. I've gotten a little older and I realize that the weight does not fall off as easy as it used to. I've got to start taking better care of my body. How about you?

As an adult I quickly learned the importance of taking care of what belongs to me, and never once did I even think to include my health in that equation. Your body is just that, yours. You are responsible for it. You dictate how well it functions. You are in charge of what goes in it. You cannot blame anyone else for what you do to your body.

> You have to be a good steward over your body. A person's body, mind and spiritual nature are all mutually dependent upon one another.

If you abuse your vehicle and do not take care of it by getting regular maintenance and keeping gas in it what will happen? It will shut down. Well the same goes for your body. If you do not watch what you eat or what you expose your body to it will shut down as well. Another area that corresponds with staying healthy and is just as important as exercise and eating healthy is sleep.

Bodies need sleep. Just as you find time in the day to do everything else, you need to make sure you are getting enough sleep. If you do not rest, your body will make you rest, one way or another.

Your body is a temple. Remember that when you think about taking care of the stuff that means the most to you. You should be on the top of that list. I've always said that if it's important to you then you will find a way to do it. Get out there and find a way to take better care of yourself. If you already have a good exercise routine, make sure you get enough rest at night. If you already do both, then make your eating habits healthier. You must never lose sight of the requirement to take care of this body that God has given you. I challenge each of you today to be in health.

Life Tools:

3 John 1:2 KJV "Beloved, I wish above all things that thou mayest prosper and be in health, even as thy soul prospereth."

1 Corinthians 6:19-20 NIV "Do you not know that your bodies are temples of the Holy Spirit, who is in you, whom you have received from God? You are not your own; you were bought at a price. Therefore honor God with your bodies."

ARE YOU A GOOD COMMUNICATOR?

I've come to learn that sometimes it's not so much what you say to people, but how you say it. This is where personalities come into play. Some people have a very straightforward personality; others are more quiet and shy. Whichever personality fits you, it is imperative that you be mindful of how you communicate.

Communication with others consists of more than just talking, it also requires listening. Listening is important because it will show you the heart of the other person. The Bible declares that out of the abundance of the heart, the mouth speaks. When you are a good listener, you are able to pin point areas you know are important, just based on their conversation. Sometimes it's best to be quiet and listen. Not everyone who talks to you is looking for feedback. Some just want a person who will be kind enough to lend an ear and hear what is on their heart.

Your communication style should fit your personality, yet still do so in a way that is loving and kind to others. It is one thing to have a strong personality, but if you are too strong you will never be able to have a healthy relationship with others. Reason being is because of your inability to set your ways to the side for just a moment for the sake of someone else. People will be intimidated by you.

You have to get to the point where you can express yourself in a nonabrasive, yet affirming manner regardless of who you are talking to. Remembering that whatever you do or say should always be in love. Words can really hurt and tear someone down. Sometimes the enemy will try to take your words and use them that very way, when you never intended it to be that way. At times I have to pray prior to, after and sometimes during my conversations with other people to cancel the assignment of the enemy to mix up my words. I also pray that God will speak through me, so that when I do open my mouth, I am not saying anything to hurt someone or cause them to take my words out of context.

I realize that miscommunication happens, but as with all things, we have to ask God to help us. Communication is a way of life. It is the key to any successful relationship, no matter what kind of relationship it is. So you must do our part to make sure you are communicating properly and effectively. The next time you are in the middle of a conversation and you don't like how things are going, stop and think for a moment. Are you a good communicator?

Life Tools:

Proverbs 15:1 NLT "A gentle answer deflects anger, but harsh words make tempers flare."

Psalms 141:3 NLT "Take control of what I say, O LORD, and guard my lips."

1 Corinthians 15:33 KJV "Be not deceived: evil communications corrupt good manners."

DON'T NEGLECT YOUR EMOTIONS

Emotions are a part of who you are. God gave you emotions when He created you, so obviously they can't be too bad. You must learn, however how not to let your emotions get the best of you. It is very easy to get caught up in the moment and just go off the deep end. You have to have self-control to remain calm, get your thoughts together, and then handle the situation accordingly. You cannot allow the cares of life to cause you to get overly emotional.

I am not saying you should ignore your emotional needs. I believe that God gave them to you for a reason. At the end of the day, you end up hurting yourself more than helping yourself by ignoring them completely. If you are feeling frustrated or aggravated don't let it fester and build up in your mind. First and foremost you must acknowledge that those feelings are not of God at all, satan is the author of confusion and frustration. Acknowledging it gives you the opportunity to use the power that God has given you to overcome. The minute you see him operating in your life, you rebuke him and send him right back to the pits of hell where he belongs. Next, you get to the root of the issue, whatever the root is. What is the bottom line behind the reason you are feeling how you feel? What is the real issue you have going on? Then lastly, deal with it. Now and days seem like it's easier for people to just brush stuff off, which in the end makes the small stuff turn into great big stuff. Whatever it is deal with it.

Communication is also a great remedy. If you feel down or discouraged, get around or talk to loved ones who you know will encourage you. Maybe you can't talk about it like you want to, try writing it down. Do whatever you need to do to express yourself. Your emotions help reveal the true matters of the heart. Acknowledge that the issue exists, dig up the root (get to the bottom of it), and deal with it. This is how you overcome.

Always remember that you are a whole person. This means body, soul and spirit. With the body, soul and spirit there has to be balance. You cannot focus on or pay more attention to one and not the others. Ask God and He will instruct you on how to be strong in all areas of your life, particularly in regards to dealing with your emotions. Whatever you do, don't neglect your emotions. With His help, you have to learn how to use everything He gave you in a manner that is pleasing unto Him.

Life Tools:

1 Corinthians 10:13 NLT "The temptations in your life are no different from what others experience. And God is faithful. He will not allow the temptation to be more than you can stand. When you are tempted, he will show you a way out so that you can endure."

Proverbs 16:32 ESV "Whoever is slow to anger is better than the mighty, and he who rules his spirit than he who takes a city."

GOD BLESS YOU!!!

I've talked before about being a blessing to others. Indeed this is very important, but right now I want to talk about being a blessing to yourself. Not so much physically, more so spiritually. The concept of reading your Bible, going to church or spending time with God in my opinion has been misconstrued. So many people do it as an obligation or requirement. This simply should not be the case. There are no laws about these things. Your love for God should prompt you to want to pray, study the word of God and serve the Lord.

God is not like man. He does not have an array of feelings He experiences everyday like we do. God is love. He is joy. He is peace. He is happiness. Yes, He desires to have a relationship with you, but if you choose not to it will not change who He is. When you spend time with God in prayer, serve in church, give to others, study the Bible and merely purpose in your heart to live righteous, you are actually blessing yourself. Your devotion to Him is the best thing you can do for yourself. I have come to learn that if you are about your Father's business, He will be about yours. In other words, when you do what you are supposed to for Him, He will make sure that all your other personal cares and concerns are taken care of.

Stop letting other people discourage you when it comes to the things of God. You do what you have to do. Better yet, you do what you know you have been called to do and what you are supposed to do. Speaking from firsthand experience, I can honestly say that the worst hurt can come from people in church. But this is why you have to stay focused. You must have a righteous mind and desire to be about the things of the Father, just like Paul. Paul was determined to do the will of the Father by any means necessary. I admire that. People talked about him, beat him, put him in jail, did everything they could to discourage him but

> God is love. He is joy. He is peace. He is happiness. Yes, He desires to have a relationship with you, but if you choose not to it will not change who He is.

Paul knew what he had been called to do and he did it. He was not distracted or discouraged by what he experienced in the flesh. He knew that his blessing was not temporary or earthly. His blessing was eternal.

So my friends, you see it is quite ok to think of yourself. Do whatever you need to do to get close to your creator. In doing so, always keep this in the back of your mind, the things on this earth are temporary, but with salvation comes everlasting life which is eternal. Bless yourself not only do you deserve it, but you need it.

Life Tools:

John 3:16 ESV ""For God so loved the world, that he gave his only Son, that whoever believes in him should not perish but have eternal life."

Proverbs 11:30-31 KJV "The fruit of the righteous is a tree of life; and he that wins souls is wise. Behold, the righteous shall be recompensed in the earth: much more the wicked and the sinner."

FIRST THINGS FIRST!!!

What are the things that seem most important in your life? What do you spend most of your time doing? I ask these two questions because a lot of times what you spend the majority of your everyday activities doing does not even involve the things that are most important to you. Family is very important, yet you spend so much of your day at work you don't really get much time with family. The busyness of today's society can sometimes make life seem like a blur. Now and days people are stressed out, feel pressured, and overall just have way too much to do. You must set priorities in life. No matter what you have going on; make time for what is important.

Before I get out of bed every morning, I always say a prayer and talk to God. I spend time with God first because I know that when I roll out of bed there is no telling what life may throw my way. My little girls make things very unpredictable for me at times. Starting your day right is a great way to help you stay on track. Talking to God and hearing what He has to say. Following the leading of the Holy Spirit inside of you all day will help you stay focused. It will also help you keep the right perspective to set priorities.

In my life, it's God first, my wonderful husband, my children then everything else has to get in where it fits in. I believe that if you set priorities in life and if you are led by God, the stress and pressures you experience will be minimal. As you build your relationship with God, you gain such an immeasurable amount of peace in your spirit that remains there at all times.

Walking hand in hand with God will allow you to enjoy every day of your life. Not just weekends or vacations. When you wake up in the morning set the tone for each day. Think about what your priorities are. If you don't have any, make some. Make it a point to do things that are not just on your to do list, but things that actually matter. Take action on stuff that has purpose and meaning. The peace that God gives will give you pleasure and relaxation even when things are not going the way you want them to. When you are in tune with Him, you will even begin to cater your schedule around Him. You will ask God what you should be doing instead of asking Him to bless what you want to do. God is just good like that. Keep God first and everything else will fall into place.

Life Tools:

Luke 12:34 KJV "For where your treasure is, there will your heart be also."

Matthew 6:33 NLT "Seek the Kingdom of God above all else, and live righteously, and he will give you everything you need."

LIFE IS A BALANCING ACT

Being busy is not always a bad thing, but for most people when they talk about it they speak on the busyness of life from a negative perspective. Really, it all depends on what you are busy doing. Whatever it is that is consuming your time, make sure that it helps you move towards fulfilling your purpose in life and is not hindering it. I spoke about priorities earlier, now I'd like to talk about balance for a moment. When there is balance, it allows you to remain upright and steady. With balance comes stability and with stability comes strength.

When going about the daily hustle and bustle of life it is essential that you have balance. A great example I'd like to share is about the many different types of food all over the world. No matter what it is, each variety of food falls into one of the different food groups. Research has shown that in order to be healthy, you should eat a certain amount of something from each food group every day. The fact is you need some of all of it, but not all of any of it. There has to be balance in order to stay healthy. If you over do any of it or under do any of it, this will have an impact on your health and the way your body functions.

Same goes for life. To have a fruitful, thriving, victorious life you must have balance. If you don't know how to balance all that you have going on, ask. God is there ready to talk to you and give you strategy on what to do. He does not want you to be all weighed down and consumed. At times I feel overwhelmed because I do have a whole lot going on. I've learned that if I put too much of my energy into one thing and not enough into something else it gets me off balance. In order for me to not feel so overwhelmed, I cannot do that. God has begun to give me different strategies and ways to make sure I focus my attention properly. I most certainly couldn't figure it out on my own. Truth be told, I still have days that are a little more cumbersome than others, but I learn from them, get up the next day and try again.

Is there an area of your life that is off balance? Doing too much of one thing, but not enough of another? Find these areas in life that need some adjustments and make them. The opportunity for things to change for the better is there. You just have to make a decision and make it happen.

Living life is like riding a bicycle. To keep your balance, you have to keep moving. Life is a balancing act, are you a good juggler?

Life Tools:

Ecclesiates 3:1- 8 NIV "There is a time for everything, and a season for every activity under the heavens: a time to be born and a time to die, a time to plant and a time to uproot, a time to kill and a time to heal, a time to tear down and a time to build, a time to weep and a time to laugh, a time to mourn and a time to dance, a time to scatter stones and a time to gather them, a time to embrace and a time to refrain from embracing, a time to search and a time to give up, a time to keep and a time to throw away, a time to tear and a time to mend, a time to be silent and a time to speak, a time to love and a time to hate, a time for war and a time for peace.

ASSET OR LIABILITY...YOU DECIDE

When you come in contact with someone, whether it's for the first time or not would you consider yourself to be an asset or liability? Most of the time when you hear these words you think about insurance, finance or investments but right now we are going to apply these concepts to life. My desire is to make an impact on this world. My desire is to be the change I want to see. My desire is to make a difference in people's life. I want to add something to every person I meet. This is what I mean by asset and liability. An asset is a useful or valuable thing, person or quality. A liability on the other hand is an obligation or debt. I'm sure you can think of that one person who only calls when they need or want something. Or that one person who every time you are around them they ask for something. I know quite a few people who fit this description and those people I would consider to be liabilities. They do not add anything to your life; instead they are constantly taking away.

Adding to someone can be as simple as always smiling when you see them or having a kind encouraging word. Exemplifying this type of behavior will cause people to be happy and excited when they are in your presence. Also, think about some of the events that have taken place throughout your lifetime, good or bad. Instead of keeping it to yourself, you can share your testimony. Sharing your experiences can either help prepare them for something that may come up in their future or help them overcome what they are already going through. You just never know. The point is however, you are pouring into them what you have on the inside of you to support them. You are adding to their life. Hopefully, when the time comes they will turn around and do the same for someone else, so the cycle will just keep going and going.

> An asset is a useful or valuable thing, person or quality. A liability on the other hand is an obligation or debt.

Think for a moment about the question I initially asked about asset or liability. Be honest in your answer. What I am talking about is the core of who you are. No one knows you better than you, this includes your motives. Not only that, but the truth of the matter no one owes you anything. You might want to take, take, take all the time because you feel you have a sense of entitlement but I promise you that if it hasn't already it will come right back around to you. As the word says, you reap what you sow. So in essence, you are only setting yourself up for failure. Bottom line, asset or liability? Do you add to those around you or are you constantly taking away? Whatever your answer is, be mindful that it's your choice.

Life Tools:

Romans 12:3-5 NLT "Because of the privilege and authority God has given me, I give each of you this warning: Don't think you are better than you really are. Be honest in your evaluation of yourselves, measuring yourselves by the faith God has given us. Just as our bodies have many parts and each part has a special function, so it is with Christ's body. We are many parts of one body, and we all belong to each other."

1 Thessalonians 5:11 ESV "Therefore encourage one another and build one another up just as you are doing."

Hebrews 10:24 NLT "Let us think of ways to motivate one another to acts of love and good works."

SOLITARY CONFINEMENT

Often times humans tend to have a fear of loneliness or isolation. As a child of Christ, what you seem to forget is that in Hebrews 13:5 the Lord your God has promised to never leave nor forsake you. Meaning, He is always there. The times when you feel like you are alone, that is the time when you need to draw closer to Him. Speak to God, tell Him how you feel and ask Him to reveal His presence to you.

Feeling lonely is not always a bad thing. It should be a time where you do a self-reflection, learn what changes need to be made or what needs to be fixed. Being lonesome also allows God to come into your life at a time when you can fully receive and accept Him. I was once told that some of the strongest and most faithful Christians are single. Why is that? This is a time in your life where you are most vulnerable.

> Being lonesome allows God to come into your life at a time when you can fully receive and accept Him.

When I was single, it seemed as though I was constantly looking for something because there was an empty void in my life that I wanted filled. There were times I actually stayed in unhealthy relationships all because of the fear of being alone and having to start all over again. How would I go from spending time with someone everyday, to not having anyone to talk to and constantly being on my own? I couldn't grasp in my mind how I was going to adjust. To my surprise however, when the time did come, I was able to get back to my first love. As I began to seek Him more and more, God stepped in and filled that empty void. He was what I was looking for all along and did not even realize it.

Being in what I like to call solitary confinement also changes your mentality. You are able to experience Christ in such an amazing and intimate way. A way that if you are surrounded by others, married and with a family you might not be as receptive to. If all you have to take care of is yourself, there is a potential for a greater focus on God and the work in which He has called you to do.

If you are single, I want to encourage you to embrace it. Let God take this time to shape and mold you for your future. God has so much in store for you. His plans are way more than you could ever imagine. He's just preparing you. God has promised that He will be with you always, even until the ends of the earth. If He brings you to something, He will most certainly bring you through it. So find peace with where you are, and know that you are never alone. Hang in there and remember what I always say, you got this, because God's got you.

LIFE TOOLS:

Hebrews 13:5 KJV "Let your conversation be without covetousness; and be content with such things as ye have: for he hath said, I will never leave thee, nor forsake thee"

Matthew 28:20 KJV "Teaching them to observe all things whatsoever I have commanded you: and, lo, I am with you alway, even unto the end of the world. Amen."

LIFE'S A JOURNEY

The beautiful thing about having a relationship with God is that it's between you and Him. No one can dictate how your relationship with Him is supposed to go. You are a unique individual; therefore your bond with your creator is going to be different. What I have come to learn is that when God sets you up to do something or gives you vision and purpose in life that is between you and Him. Some people are not going to understand because, guess what? They aren't supposed to. Therefore, do not expect everyone to be on the same page and understand what He's doing in your life, no matter how bad you may want them to. When you are obedient to God, some family, close friends and even church folk may think you are crazy. Some might even judge you or have some not so nice things to say. In spite of your connection to them, you must be willing to put their thoughts and feelings aside and trust in your Heavenly Father. Trust what He is doing in you and know that you are headed in the right direction. In order to reach your destination however, you must keep moving. A journey is not a journey once you stop moving. The Lord knows all things, and as you go from season to season allow Him to reveal the plans He has for your life. Once He does, do not allow anyone to stop you from accomplishing just that.

Have you been struggling with being in the will of God and doing what you know you have been called to do? I want to encourage you to do a thorough examination of your present situation. Make up in your mind that you are willing and ready to do whatever it takes. A lot of times in life people come to a stumbling block where they are forced to make decisions they aren't ready to make or don't want to make. Make a decision. It's easy to say what you are not going to do, but you must decide what you are going to do. Once you do that, rid your thoughts of the negative talk

> When God sets you up to do something or gives you vision and purpose in life that is between you and Him. Some people are not going to understand because, guess what? They aren't supposed to.

of other people around you. If you have to, just keep some things to yourself. Let your actions do the talking for you. People are going to talk regardless; you just can't let it stop you.

God is doing some stuff in your life right now. Stuff that you don't understand. Stuff that you don't like. Stuff that even hurts you to your heart. My brothers and sisters in Christ, I am here to tell you it's ok. All of the "stuff" you are going through is working together for your good and for God's glory. Seasons change, people change but the word of God stays the same. No matter how bad it hurts, remember it is all apart of life's journey.

Bottom line; don't expect everyone to understand your journey, especially if they've never had to walk your path. You must be like King David and keep looking to the hills from whence cometh your help, because your help does not come from man, it comes from God. Remember, there is no turning back on your life's journey, just make new paths to follow instead.

Life Tools:

Jeremiah 29:11 NIV "For I know the plans I have for you," declares the LORD, "plans to prosper you and not to harm you, plans to give you hope and a future."

Romans 8:37-39 KJV "No, in all these things we are more than conquerors through him that loved us. For I am persuaded, that neither death, nor life, nor angels, nor principalities, nor powers, nor things present, nor things to come, Nor height, nor depth, nor any other creature, shall be able to separate us from the love of God, which is in Christ Jesus our Lord."

Psalms 121:1-2 KJV "I will lift up my eyes to the hills, from where comes my help. My help comes from the LORD, which made heaven and earth"

LEAVE THE PAST RIGHT WHERE IT IS

Social status and titles mean very little to me because difficulties in life show no mercy based on who you are or who you know. No matter how you look at it, life is not easy. Nor, do I think it was ever intended to be. I've learned and am still learning that there will be some things in my life that don't go the way I want, but I can't just throw in the towel. I have to make a decision to focus on the positive and live a life of joy and happiness in spite of my past or what I may be experiencing in my present.

Living thousands of miles away from my closest friends and family, I experienced different times off and on of being homesick. My mom and aunt came to visit and I felt like it would be a great time for me to get the encouragement I needed to help me get through my last stretch of living overseas. Their visit went better than I could have ever imagined, however when they left I felt some kind of way. I did not realize that I would miss them so much and instead of getting the push I needed, the enemy tried to attack my mind and get me to revert back to how I felt when I first got here.

I had to call upon the strength of God deep down inside of me to get me back on track, forget all about my past feelings and focus on my present. I made the decision to focus on those choices that I can affect and continue to make my life worth living. While I still missed my family, I had to make the choice to live my life to fullest each and every day. I decided that I would not allow how I felt to get me off focus and regress back to my past behavior. I knew that I had purpose right where I was and in spite of everything, I must finish the race that God had set before me.

> If you spend so much time focusing on moments, situations or circumstances from the past, you just might miss the awesome things that God is doing right in front of you or any special moments that are to come.

This is just one example I am sharing. I'm sure you could think of several things you have experienced that maybe did not go the way you want it to go or maybe caused you hurt and pain. I want to encourage you today. Whatever it is you are feeling I am here to say that you can triumph over the challenges and difficulties of life. It's all about your outlook, strength of character and determination. You simply have to choose. Call upon your faith and trust in God to help you keep walking toward a better future. Leave your past behind you. This even includes past behaviors. If you spend so much time focusing on moments, situations or circumstances from the past, you just might miss the awesome things that God is doing right in front of you or any special moments that are to come. Learn from it, grow from it but leave your past right where it is. Do not try to take it into your present or the future.

Life Tools:

Philippians 3:13-14 KJV "Brothers, I count not myself to have apprehended: but this one thing I do, forgetting those things which are behind, and reaching forth to those things which are before, I press toward the mark for the prize of the high calling of God in Christ Jesus."

2 Corinthians 5:17 KJV "Therefore if any man be in Christ, he is a new creature: old things are passed away; behold, all things are become new."

OBEDIENCE IS BEST

I am a firm believer that when you know better you do better. That being said, lately I have wondered why so many people still choose to do the wrong thing. I mean every time I turn on the television or go on the internet, the amount of ruthless and outright disobedient behavior is unbelievable. I was having a conversation the other day about people's rights and the laws of the land. Yes, I get that there are laws and rights, a lot of which I feel like if they did not exist people would still do what they want to do anyway. But even still, just because you have the right to do something, does not make it the right thing to do. We are experiencing a severe moral decline in our society. People know better, but seem to be doing whatever it is they are big and bad enough to do. And the more unfortunate part about it is a lot of these same people also profess Christianity. As a Christian you are to be in the world, but not be of the world. In other words, you cannot do what everyone else is doing just because everyone else is doing it. You have to set the standard.

Christians are held to a different norm. Those of the world run their own lives. They do what they want, when they want without regard for how it affects others. They most certainly are not concerned with whether or not their actions are approved of by God. Christians however, should seek to walk in obedience. Not obedience to man, but to God. They are to be led, guided and willingly controlled by the Holy Spirit because the Holy Spirit will always lead right to the will of God.

God wants you to choose His will, but what He won't do is force it upon you. So saying 'when you know better you do better' this is just not a completely true statement. The fact of the matter is you must still make a decision. When you know better, you must decide to do better. This is why so many people are doing anything they want. They are making a decision.

The fact of the matter is obedience hurts. It is the place where your flesh and your spirit disconnect. When your feelings do not support your actions, it can be a difficult thing to process. So, in essence obedience is a form of strength. How strong are you when you just do what you want to do? It takes self-control, discipline and commitment to actually do the right thing.

I've made it up in my mind that I am going to be like Paul and run my race and finish my course. When life happens, I will be obedient and I hope you will too. My prayer is that the spirit of God inside of me will lead me and guide me at all times. When you willfully choose to do what God requires of you, even when your thoughts and feelings are not supporting it, it shows your love for God. No matter what life throws your way, make up in your mind right now that you will be obedient.

Life Tools:

John 14:15 NLT ""If you love me, obey my commandments."

Romans 2:13 NLT "For merely listening to the law doesn't make us right with God. It is obeying the law that makes us right in his sight."

BLOOD IS THICKER THAN WATER....OR IS IT?

Growing up, I've always had a very tight knit and close family. My mother has seven siblings, all of whom live in the same city. Holidays, birthdays, graduations, any type of celebration you can think of was always such a big event within our family because we all came together to show love and have a good time. To this very day, my family is still extremely close and I wouldn't trade any of them for the world. That being said, I have also come to learn that not everybody's family is like mine. Some people don't have close relationships with their parents, siblings, aunts, uncles or cousins. Some people come from a small family and most of them have passed away. Others come from families that have been separated. Whatever the structure is, all families are different which got me to thinking about the phrase "blood is thicker than water". What that has always meant to me is that family sticks together and you never let someone who is not apart of the family come in and tear it apart. Ok this sounds good, but truth is some people who may not be your blood will treat you better and love you more than any blood relative you have.

Family is not always blood. True family is those individuals in your life who want you in theirs, the ones who accept you for who you are. Individuals who would do anything just to put a smile on your face and who love you no matter what. If you have people that God has placed in your life who may not be related to you, but who are concerned about your well-being and who have welcomed you into their life with open arms, you are blessed. If they love on you and treat you with sincere compassion and kindness, thank God for them. These people are what I like to call divine connections and they are heaven sent by God to show you just how much He cares for you.

> True family is those individuals in your life who want you in theirs, the ones who accept you for who you are. They are individuals who would do anything just to put a smile on your face and who love you no matter what.

I consider myself blessed because I have the best of both worlds. A loving, fun, down to earth family who I know only wants what's best for me and has my back no matter what. I also have a few people in my life who I know have been sent as divine connections, to further exemplify the love that God has for me.

God shows His love to you in so many amazing ways. Yes, He provides the physical needs in your life such as food, shelter, clothes, etc. But it's the other small things that you sometimes take for granted such as relationships that He is also concerned with. Some people will hurt you, but you must remember that not everyone is like that. There are a few people that God will send your way just to bless you. They will always encourage, lift up and support you in such a way that you know it's nobody but Him.

Thank God for your family, those who are blood relatives and those who are not. Either way you look at it there will always be a select group of people you hold near and dear to your heart. Keep it that way. These are the people who are going to make this journey called life a lot more endurable. So the phrase "blood is thicker than water" may or may not always be the case. The reality is it does not matter. Stick with those who are for you. Stay connected with people who have your best interest at heart. And who are overall concerned about your well-being. Anyone who does not meet the required criteria, relative or not, do not deserve a place in your life.

Life Tools:

1 Corinthians 13:4-7 NLT "Love is patient and kind. Love is not jealous or boastful or proud or rude. It does not demand its own way. It is not irritable, and it keeps no record of being wronged. It does not rejoice about injustice but rejoices whenever the truth wins out. Love never gives up, never loses faith, is always hopeful, and endures through every circumstance."

Psalms 103:17 NIV "But from everlasting to everlasting the LORD's love is with those who fear him, and his righteousness with their children's children"

IS IT POSSIBLE TO TRUST EVEN WHEN YOU DON'T UNDERSTAND?

Is it possible to trust, even when you do not understand? The initial response for most people would be no. We have a tendency to want to know everything before the word trust can be applied. In actuality however, there are a lot of areas in your everyday life where you trust and have no clear understanding at all. For instance, you get into your car every day and drive it, not understanding how everything under the hood works. You trust the car enough to get in and go so you can reach your destination. This same theory is true for when you sit down on a chair. You may not understand what the chair is made of or how it was constructed, but you trust it enough to sit down on it in hopes that it will hold you up and keep you off the ground. The second trust is broken it is very, very hard to get back. It's like a crisp clean sheet of paper. Once that paper is crumbled up, it is close to impossible to ever get it back to that same crisp sheet it once was.

Taking all of this into consideration, why is it so hard then to trust the one who created all things? Why are you hesitant to trust the one who formed heaven and earth, trees, cars, chairs and even humans? In my opinion people have such a hard time trusting God because a lot of times they cannot comprehend or understand what He is doing. You trust the chair, even though you've seen it fall on the ground several times. You trust your friends, even though they have let you down in the past. You trust the bank even though they are making money off of your money. You trust everything else more than you trust God. Yet, God has never ever failed you and your trust in Him does not come quite as easy. If nothing else, look at His track record. It's solid. Every time you have been through a storm in life you have come out. In spite of every storm, heartache, pain or disappointment, by the grace of God you made it through.

In Isaiah 55, the Lord declares that His ways are not our ways and His thoughts are not our thoughts. In essence that means there are going to be quite a few things you do not understand in this life. Never let your inability to understand turn into distrust and you trying to take matters into your own hands. Love is trust and if you really love God like you say you do, then you must trust His plan even when you don't understand. Trust that you are where God intended for you to be at this very moment. Every experience, good or bad, is all apart of His divine plan for your life. Planning and preparation are good, but doing so without the peace of God is not. In other words, when you make your plans, if those plans do not go quite as you intended you should still have peace and know that it's going just the way God intended for it to.

Christians are called believers. Ironically however, most Christians are more like unbelieving believers. God wants to be number one in your life. He wants you to put your confidence and trust in Him, all the time, in everything. You may not understand what is happening in your life. It may be craziness all around you. It is times like these where your declaration of trust is put to the test. You say you trust God, but do you really? Your lights have been cut off, it's the weekend and you know you paid your bill. Do you trust Him? You go to work early, stay late and have excellent reports from your superiors yet they give the promotion to someone else. Do you still trust Him? You lose your spouse then two days later your parent. Do you still trust? These are all situations that if you haven't already had to deal with, it could come knocking at your door any day. Will the love you have for God and the trust you talk about rise to the occasion?

Is it possible to trust even when you do not understand? Absolutely. You just have to have an intimate relationship with your creator so if and when the time does come, you can rely on His strength inside of you to make it through and not your own. I challenge you to make a choice. Decide today that you will trust God no matter what, especially when you do not understand.

Life Tools:

Proverbs 3:5-6 NKJV "Trust in the LORD with all your heart, And lean not on your own understanding; In all your ways acknowledge Him, And He shall direct your paths."

Isaiah 55:8 NIV "For my thoughts are not your thoughts, neither are your ways my ways," declares the LORD."

Jeremiah 17:5-9 NIV "This is what the LORD says: "Cursed is the one who trusts in man, who draws strength from mere flesh and whose heart turns away from the LORD. That person will be like a bush in the wastelands; they will not see prosperity when it comes.

They will dwell in the parched places of the desert, in a salt land where no one lives. "But blessed is the one who trusts in the LORD, whose confidence is in him. They will be like a tree planted by the water that sends out its roots by the stream. It does not fear when heat comes; its leaves are always green. It has no worries in a year of drought and never fails to bear fruit." The heart is deceitful above all things and beyond cure. Who can understand it?"

IF YOU MADE IT, THEY CAN TOO

Do not ever be ashamed of who you are, where you are from or what you have been through. Everybody has a story, and that story is what makes each person unique and an individual. Sometimes you may feel as though you do not want to share your story, thinking that no one will care. What you have to realize however is that indeed, some people may not care, but there are some people who will care and your story could help someone else. In all honesty, I've come to learn that what you went through in life is for someone else. The storms, trials and tribulations you face are only temporary. Once they are over you move forward. By sharing your story you help someone else move forward as well.

The Bible declares that we overcome by the blood and of the lamb and the word of our testimony. This means that if you are to truly be victorious and overcome the troubles of life, you have to share your testimony with others. God showed me this a while ago when I was at a very dark place in life. It seemed as though hardship and suffering lived on my doorstep and I really did not know how I was going to make it. It was by the grace of God that I did. Surprisingly to me however, when I did almost immediately He began to send people to me that were going through some of the same things I had been through. People I didn't even really know very well or who I had only spoken with maybe once or twice, basically complete strangers. They would always say that for some reason they felt compelled to talk to me. This is when I knew that what I had been through was not just for me. The pain, hurt and setback that I endured was a tool He wanted me to use for ministry. Who better to encourage than people who I could relate to? People who I understood their story, because it was so similar to mine. We shared something in common. I quickly learned that when dealt with the right way, in the end these encounters were for my good but more so for His glory.

Another side of this issue is that far too many people expend tremendous energy to hide their pain, health problems or troubles just to function in this world. Why this is so, I do not know. Either they are ashamed or don't feel strong enough to be honest or maybe it's a little of both. Bottom line, you simply never know what someone is going through. Some people wear their hard times on their shoulders and want to complain and tell the whole world about it, but a lot of people do not. Think about this the next time you are ready to laugh or point the finger at someone. Instead, make a decision to be kind because truth be told we are all fighting some kind of battle.

The highs and lows, ups and downs should all be considered a beautiful thing. Life may not be perfect, but it is beautiful. Life is not fair, but God is. A lot of people say they want to be used by God, and here is a perfect way to do so. The next time someone comes to you broken, be the glue to help them get it back together. Be transparent with them and show some compassion. We are quick to share the good, now let's flip the script and share the bad too. This will for sure make the devil mad. As you encourage people, let them know that if you made it, they can too.

Life Tools:

Revelation 12:11 KJV "And they overcame him by the blood of the Lamb, and by the word of their testimony; and they loved not their lives unto the death."

Mark 5:19 ESV "And he did not permit him but said to him, "Go home to your friends and tell them how much the Lord has done for you, and how he has had mercy on you."

WE MUST STICK TOGETHER

There is power in agreement. I am not talking about people who agree with you per se. I am talking about people who will stand with you to support you at all times. I am talking about those who will stick with you through thick and thin, good or bad and who will not betray you or judge you. If more people would realize this, thinking of themselves less and others more the world would really be a better place.

One of the best and simplest ways to determine who's who and what's what is to go through something. This is when you find out the real character of those around you. People are generally all for you when everything is smooth sailing. Let a little storm come and that's when the rubber meets the road. When this happens

One of the best and simplest ways to determine who's who and what's what is to go through something. This is when you find out the real character of those around you.

and folks show you who they really are, believe them. Do not base your relationship with anyone upon words. Let it be the action that comes behind those words that determines whether or not they deserve a role in your life. When you find somebody good, stick with them. Either way it goes, learn from other people's behavior.

The Bible speaks of the power that comes when people of faith can get together on one accord. I've been a loner for majority of my life, but as I've grown wiser I have also come to understand the power that comes with agreement. The power behind having people who you can talk with, pray with, and just be yourself. These are those divine connections I was talking about before. Some of these people may be family and some may be friends. Whatever title they have in your life, they make you a better you. When you are sad or finding it hard to have faith in a storm, you can connect to those people and they will have faith for you to help you get through. Then when you bounce back, the roles can reverse and they might need to rely on your faith to get through their hard time. This is what I mean by sticking together and the power that comes with it. The enemy would have you to be isolated, especially from other believers. Why is this? Because you tend to be weaker in your struggles when you are alone. When you are connected to people who help lift you up those sad days are cut short. In result, you are then able to shut down the enemy and focus more on fulfilling the plans and purposes that God has for your life.

Yeah it may be hard to let people in your life, especially after being hurt. I am here to tell you once you have the right folks in your corner, you will be so much stronger. Think about it, even Jesus had a small group of select individuals that He stuck with. All of which played a vital role in His life here on earth. The body of Christ must learn to stick together. You may not get along with everyone, but with the help of God you will find a select few who when yall come together there will be so much power in your union. Remember, one can chase one thousand but two can chase ten thousand. By staying connected, you are more effective. There is only so much you can do by yourself. Besides, God never intended for you to take the journey of life all alone anyway. If He had, you think He would have created all of us?

Life Tools:

Deuteronomy 32:20 KJV "How should one chase a thousand, and two put ten thousand to flight, except their Rock had sold them, and the LORD had shut them up?"

Matthew 18:19 NIV "Again, truly I tell you that if two of you on earth agree about anything they ask for, it will be done for them by my Father in heaven."

YOU GOT THIS, 'CAUSE GOD'S GOT YOU!

Finding purpose in life can sometimes take a while but once you do, things seem to be so much more meaningful. When you figure out what you are supposed to be doing, it gives you an opportunity to have clear and succinct goals. The most beautiful thing about it is that it gives you something to believe in. You are now able to have dreams and a vision for your life. Right now, I want to encourage you to believe.

The same time you find your purpose and set goals for yourself, you better believe the enemy is ready to do everything he can to shut you down. That's his job, so expect it. But instead of allowing his tactics to prevent you from being triumphant, reverse things up a little

> When the enemy comes to attack let it be a form of confirmation letting you know that you are headed in the right direction. The devil is not going to fight those who are on his side. He comes after God's people because we are his enemy, just as he is ours.

and use it as fuel to ignite a fire inside of you that will thrust you towards what you believe in.

When the enemy comes to attack let it be a form of confirmation letting you know that you are headed in the right direction. The devil is not going to fight those who are on his side. He comes after God's people because we are his enemy, just as he is ours. It can hurt at first, mostly because it catches you off guard but once you fully dissect the situation for what it is, you will quickly find the root of the issue. You see, satan already knows the wonderful and great things that God created you for. He has literally peeked into your future. His job is to do everything in his power to stop that future from coming to fruition. It's up to you however, to not let him. You have to make up in your mind that come hell or high water, you are not going to allow the enemy to defeat you.

God uses people and so does the devil. Never let someone who gave up on their dreams talk you out of going after yours. Never let negative comments or quick judgments discourage you. Things may get tough and at times may be a bit crazy but stay committed. Matter fact, before you even get started make a covenant with God that as long as He sustains you will be committed to Him in whatever it is He has for you to do. Don't expect to do it on your own. You will need the strength of God to endure, I promise you. Hang in there, keep the faith and most importantly never stop believing. You got this, because God's got you!

Life Tools:

Philippians 4:12-13 NASB "I know how to get along with humble means, and I also know how to live in prosperity; in any and every circumstance I have learned the secret of being filled and going hungry, both of having abundance and suffering need. I can do all things through Him who strengthens me..."

Isaiah 41:10 NLT "Don't be afraid, for I am with you. Don't be discouraged, for I am your God. I will strengthen you and help you. I will hold you up with my victorious right hand."

LET IT RAIN

No matter how much you may dislike the rain, you have to admit it serves a purpose. I used to really despise rainy days because it seemed more like a huge inconvenience to me. Trying to pull the umbrella out while carrying grocery bags, and hurrying two children in the house. That's just too much, ugh! Today however, as I sat inside and watched the rain I began to reflect a little. I may think that the rain is an inconvenience, but truth is we need the rain. The rain is what makes the flowers so pretty and full; it's what causes the grass to be so beautiful and green. The rain is what fills the lakes and rivers. The sound and sight of the heavens washing away the dirt and dust of the world is just so relaxing.

Now thinking from a more spiritual perspective, when you talk about the storms of life it is not usually a good thing. It is typically describing a tough situation or season of hardship. Just like an actual rainstorm however, when the storms of life knock on your door, you must have the strength deep down inside to see the good that can come out of it. Very few people experience pain and heartache, or any type of distress and not come out stronger in the end. It's something about going through that process that can literally make or break you. And if it breaks you, get prepared to do it all over again. Just a little side note, could that be why you keep going through the same thing over and over and over? It's time you make a decision to deal with it the right way. Stop walking around the mountain and walk on into your promised land.

When passing through the storms of life, that's right passing through not staying there, you have to be tough and remain strong. Focus not so much on what you can't do, but more on what you can do. What is in your control? Once you figure that out, do something about it. You do the natural, which will allow God to do the super. You must do your part.

You do the natural, which will allow God to do the super. You must do your part.

Instead of getting down and upset when the tough times come your way, change your perspective a little. Think about it like this, things could always be worse. If they are bad now it only means things will get better. The Eagle is one of the most beautiful animals in all creation. Not just their physical appearance but the ability that God placed inside of them is what I love. Most other birds fly to get away from the storm and seek shelter. An Eagle however, avoids the storm by simply rising above it. In the storms of life, you have to take on the heart and mind of an Eagle.

Approach your troubles by rising above them. Don't take the easy road, take the high road. It may take a little more work and determination to get you there, but in the end it will most certainly be worth it. The next time a storm is headed your way, take a moment for self-reflection then respond accordingly. This is your opportunity for the spirit of God to rise up on the inside of you. Show the world who you are and more importantly, who's you are. Instead of running from the storm, let the rain come and spread those royal wings and fly above it.

Life Tools:

Psalms 91:1-16 NIV "Whoever dwells in the shelter of the Most High will rest in the shadow of the Almighty will say of the Lord, "He is my refuge and my fortress, my God, I n whom I trust." Surely he will save you from the fowler's snare and from the deadly pestilence. He will cover you with his feathers, and under his wings you will find refuge; his faithfulness will be your shield and rampart. You will not fear the terror of night, nor the arrow that flies by day, nor the pestilence that stalks in the darkness, nor the plague that destroys at midday. A thousand may fall at your side, ten thousand at your right hand, but it will not come near you. You will only observe with your eyes and see the punishment of the wicked. If you say, "The Lord is my refuge, and you make the Most High your dwelling, no harm will overtake you, no disaster will come near your tent. For he will command his angels concerning you to guard you in all your ways; they will lift you up in their hands, so that you will not strike your foot against a stone. You will tread on the lion and the cobra; you will trample the great lion and the serpent. "Because he loves me," says the Lord, "I will rescue him; I will protect him, for he acknowledges my name. He will call on me, and I will answer him; I will be with him in trouble, I will deliver him and honor him. With long life I will satisfy him and show him my salvation."

COMMIT TO BEING COMMITTED

Ever been around someone who every other week comes up with these "bright" ideas? One week they are going to open a car wash, the next week they're creating a new computer program, then the week after that they're selling magazines. Why don't you make up your mind what you are going to do, then stick to it? People like this bother me, not because they are always coming up with ways to make money, but because they are not committed. If they would simply commit themselves to something, whatever something they choose they'd have a much better chance at succeeding instead of dibbling and dabbling in a little bit of this and a little bit of that. I am all for being well rounded, but perfect one thing at a time. Besides, everything is not for you. Know the areas you are gifted and talented in and stick to it.

Our society has become what I like to call a microwave society. You want everything quick, fast and in a hurry. Yet, aren't willing to do the work to make it happen. There has to be a level of commitment in every area of your life. Commitment to your family, your job, just your overall well-being. Certain things are just not going to happen overnight. Your level of commitment has to be as such that no matter how long it takes; you are going to give it everything you have until it comes to pass.

You should first and foremost commit your ways to the Lord. Let everything you do be in honor to God. The Bible declares that in all of your ways you are to acknowledge Him. Doing so, I believe will steer you in the right direction. Now don't get me wrong, being fully committed does have some challenges. Life has struggles period. When you are committed however it just seems like those struggles are magnified because they take away from whatever it is you are trying to do.

Whether it is being committed in a relationship or being committed on your job, there will be times where you stop and think if all your hard work is even worth it. This is where allowing God to steer you in the right direction comes into the picture. If you know that you are in the will of God, you will have a lot more peace about everything. In moments such as these, I also want you to think about why you even started in the first place. This is always the best motivating factor for me, because I know if I start something I am doing so for a reason. If I can get my mind back to that original place when it all begin, that gives me the bump I need to get back on track.

Be mindful of what you commit yourself to. Certain things are not worth your time. You must not allow the enemy to come in and distract you. Do not allow the devil to get you off course for what God has called you to do. When you have a vision or dream about life, be sure that your vision surpasses your resources so that you can always live a life of faith. Being committed requires a great deal of faith. While you are busy doing the work, you really do not know what the end result will be. You may have some idea of how you want it to turn out, but you really just never know. There has to be some sort of deep-rooted faith inside of you that will give you the motivation you need to keep going.

Commitment is a sign of growth and maturity. As mentioned earlier, if you want to be successful in life you have to be willing to commit yourself to something. If you want to be a successful mother, you have to commit yourself to your family. If you want to be a successful manager at work, you must commit yourself to learning the job. True success requires true commitment. Are you committed?

Life Tools:

Psalms 37:5 NLT "Commit everything you do to the LORD. Trust him, and he will help you."

Numbers 23:19 KJV "God is not a man, that he should lie; neither the son of man, that he should repent: hath he said, and shall he not do it? or hath he spoken, and shall he not make it good?"

TAKE A BREAK...YOU DESERVE IT

I know the issues of life keep you going day in and day out, but everybody deserves a break every now and then. Take some time for yourself. Do something you enjoy like read a book or get a massage. Sometimes you really have to just slow down and take some time for yourself. For me personally, taking time to myself doesn't even require me to do much. If I just sit in a room alone in silence and read a book I am happy. Some people like to do things and go places, and that's all fine too. Do whatever makes you happy. The point is, do something. As adults we have a lot of daily obligations, so whatever your something is just make sure that it takes you away from the regular norms in life.

I've learned that from time to time your regular routine can get the best of you. What I mean is it can wear you out. You go to work, run errands, cook dinner, have family time, get the kids ready for bed and not to mention any other extracurricular activities you have going on. These are all perfectly normal, but there comes a point in time when you just need a break.

What a break does for me is allows me to actually enjoy the moment that I am in. There are no obligations or time restraints. I am able to simply relax. Seems like at times you can get so busy preparing for one thing or fixing another, you actually miss out on what's right in front you at that very moment. The duties are always going to be there. Taking a break could actually help you to complete those duties. Here's why I say that, instead of being stressed and overwhelmed, it gives you time to calm down and get your head together.

Taking a break allows your body to be refueled. You give so much of yourself day in and day out that you become totally depleted. Taking the time to just chill, gives you the opportunity to be filled back up. I know this to be true spiritually as well. When you are constantly ministering, praying for people, counseling, etc. you just pour more and more of yourself out. Stepping back for a moment and taking rest in God is what you need to be filled up again. Allowing the opportunity for God to pour Himself into you even the more will give you the wherewithal to continue to do what He has called you to do for the people.

So take rest. Remember, a field that has rested yields a bountiful crop.

Life Tools:

Psalms 37:7 KJV "Rest in the LORD, and wait patiently for him: fret not thyself because of him who prospereth in his way, because of the man who bringeth wicked devices to pass."

Matthew 11:28-30 NLT " Then Jesus said, "Come to me, all of you who are weary and carry heavy burdens, and I will give you rest. Take my yoke upon you. Let me teach you, because I am humble and gentle at heart, and you will find rest for your souls. For my yoke is easy to bear, and the burden I give you is light."

GO FOR IT!

What is it that motivates you to keep going? What motivates you to try something new? I hate to say it, but the more I talk to other people, the more they seem to be motivated by the wrong things. Now and days celebrities; musicians, actors, talk show hosts, pretty much anyone who has a few dollars and is put in front of the camera has become the object of attention for most. They look up to these people as if they make the world go around when in actuality a lot of the "celebrities" are just putting up a facade while the camera is running anyway. In essence, people admire something that is fake. They talk about Bentley's and a few of them may even drive them, but you do not know what they had to go through to get it.

Instead of being enthused by what the world sees as being rich, why not change your perspective of what rich is.

Instead of being enthused by what the world sees as being rich, why not change your perspective of what rich is. Rich does not have to have anything to do with money. Rich can mean happy, at peace, calm, stress free or worry free. All of which sound good to me. I guarantee you if you ask the people who do have a lot of money they don't have any of these things. It is very unfortunate because some people are so poor that all they have is money.

Stop looking at these people as motivation and look to God. He is the billionaire of all billionaires. He has all the money in the world, and He also has peace, joy, love, happiness and the list could go on and on. He has everything because He is God. You must stop looking to the things of the world to find what God has already placed inside of you. Be motivated by the love He has for you, His child and the plans and purposes in which He created for your life.

It is so easy to be distracted by the things you see on T.V. or read on the internet, so stay focused. Everyone who has ever been successful at anything had to get up, get out there and just do it. They put on their pants one leg at a time just like you do. So don't think it strange or even impossible for you to do great things. You are a child of the King and above all else, you have the favor of God on your life. If you keep saying to yourself there is more to life than this, you are absolutely right. There is a whole lot more to life than what you see in front of you. Turn the TV off, log out of Facebook, and go for it. I dare you.

Life Tools:

Philippians 2:13 NLT "For God is working in you, giving you the desire and the power to do what pleases him."

Philippians 4:13 KJV "I can do all things through Christ which strengtheneth me."

SHIFT

Ladies and gentlemen, boys and girls all over the world....it's time to shift! Shift your mindset and shift the way you go about doing things. The definition of being insane is doing the same thing over and over and expecting different results. Have you been expecting or wanting some changes in your life? If so, what are you doing? If you're merely sitting around waiting for things to just magically happen then guess what, you probably gone be sitting there for a while. Shift!

In order for change to come, a shift must take place. Shift the way you think and I guarantee you shifting the way you do things will happen automatically. I say that speaking from personal experience. I had been in a situation that mentally I couldn't find any good in, knowing that God put me there. My mindset was extremely negative. I spoke negatively about my situation. I also allowed others to speak negativity into my life about the situation. God could not do what He wanted to do with me until I shifted my way of thinking. Immediately when I shifted my state of mind, the way I did things totally changed. Shift!

I want to elaborate on your thoughts for just a moment. Far too often people have a tendency to stay stuck on all the things they've have done wrong in life. Shift! We are all humans. No one is perfect, we all make mistakes. A shift takes place when you are able to pick up the lessons learned from the previous chapter, all while looking straight ahead and writing a new chapter in life. Instead of beating yourself up for your mistakes, get over it. That's right, get over it! Focus the majority of your energy and attention on what you have done right. Whatever you are doing right, keep doing it. Matter fact, take it up a notch. Perfect those right things and make it a point to operate in excellence. Shift!

A slight change in position, direction or tendency could be the very thing that God is waiting on. If you have an expectancy of change, that's something that God has placed on the inside of you. Remember, nothing is going to change if you keep doing the same thing. What is it that needs to change in order for you to get those things you are expecting? God is waiting on you to do your part. This requires you to do what? Shift! Alright, now I hope you got it. So let's go make some moves. In order for you to change the world, you have to get yourself together first. Be the change you want to see. Shift!

Life Tools:

Romans 12:2 NLT "Don't copy the behavior and customs of this world, but let God transform you into a new person by changing the way you think. Then you will learn to know God's will for you, which is good and pleasing and perfect."

Ephesians 2:10 NIV "For we are God's handiwork, created in Christ Jesus to do good works, which God prepared in advance for us to do"

DECISIONS, DECISIONS, DECISIONS... CONSEQUENCES, CONSEQUENCES, CONSEQUENCES

As I reflect upon where I am today in life, I can honestly see the reality of consequences. Yes, I've made a lot of mistakes. I did some stupid stuff growing up. On the flip side however, I made a lot of good decisions. There are some things that I actually got right. Looking into the big beautiful eyes of my two little girls reminds me of that each and every day.

Typically, when you think of consequences, you think of negative results based on decisions that are made. In fact, when I looked up words that are synonymous with 'consequences' there are words like penalty and cost included in the list. The result or effect of an action is how you define consequence. Nowhere does it say that result or effect has to be negative.

So what, you've made some bad decisions, we all have. What about those decisions you made that were right? So seldom you fail to give yourself credit for the things you actually did right. These right decisions have consequences as well.

Say you decide to give a homeless man on the street a hot meal; you better believe there is no penalty in that. This is where the law of reciprocity comes into play. You are blessed to be a blessing. When you make the decision to bless someone else, the consequence will be that you will be blessed as well.

The place you need to avoid is being in the valley of indecision. Yes, you make bad decisions and you make good ones. Both of these are required in order to move forward in life. However, when you are stuck in a valley of indecision there are consequences for that also. There is such an unsettling that comes behind not making a decision or even worse, letting someone else make the decision for you. Whether it's a big decision like where you are going to live or something small like what you are going to eat for dinner, you decide.

> You've made some bad decisions, we all have. What about those decisions you made that were right? So seldom you fail to give yourself credit for the things you actually did right.

I truly believe that decisions have a tremendous impact on your life and maintaining the ability to reach your destiny. You face some tough situations in life, which can make it very difficult to make decisions on your own. This is where your foundation comes into play. You must take heed to the word of God at all times. The Bible says that in all of our ways we are to acknowledge God. Whether they are difficult or easy so to speak, you should be seeking Him about these decisions anyway.

The next time you are placed in a position where you have to make a decision take a minute to think about what the consequences may be. You know there will be some. The end result of decisions is consequences. Just remember that those consequences are not always bad. When you do good, good things come to you. Either way, take a moment to reflect and hear from God before you move forward.

Life Tools:

Proverbs 3:5-6 NIV "Trust in the LORD with all your heart and lean not on your own understanding; in all your ways submit to him, and he will make your paths straight."

Galatians 6:7 KJV "Be not deceived; God is not mocked: for whatsoever a man soweth, that shall he also reap."

BE EMPOWERED

It's time for you to start empowering yourself. Stop sitting around looking for other people to do stuff for you. Get up, get out, and get something. There was a time in my life where I wanted to take the easy way out. If there was a shortcut or alternative way to accomplishing something, I took it. Why? Because truth is, I was just trying to get what I wanted quickly and not really put in the work. If I could let someone else do the work for me and I still get what I want, then so be it. In my mind, this was all a part of being independent. This may still be the work ethic of some, but by doing this you will never fully learn how to appreciate what you have when you get it.

What does it mean to be empowered? It means putting in the work. Work could mean studying, doing research or it could mean simply coming up with a strategy to accomplish a goal and doing it. To put in the work however, you have to have goals. There has to be an objective that you are trying to reach. So the first step to becoming empowered is figuring out what your objective is.

What are your goals? Long term? Short term? Immediate? A lot of times you get so caught up with life that you don't really think about goals. You just focus on making it day by day. Goals are essential. Having a goal is simply stating what your aim or desired result is for that particular area. You should have family goals, financial goals, career goals, and personal goals. Set goals for every aspect of your life. Basically, anything that you commit your time to should have a goal.

When you set goals, you empower yourself because now you are looking to no one other than yourself to accomplish these goals. When you have a desired result in mind, it will help you stay focused. You can be easily distracted when life happens, as it so often does. Having goals helps bring things back into perspective for you. It helps you get your mind back together. When you get your mind right, you are then able to operate in the power that God has placed on the inside of you. This will push you to work hard to accomplish your goal, even in those times when you don't feel like it.

You can apply the principle of being empowered spiritually by knowing your word. The word of God is what gives you the focus and discipline you need to live a life that is pleasing and acceptable in the sight of God. A life that is righteous and holy. The word is what gives you not only power, but strength to overcome the enemy. Having the word of God inside of you gives you confidence; it is the blueprint for life. It will revolutionize your entire perspective on life.

Empower yourself. Use the tools given to you and do something with them. As children of the Most High God, defeat is not an option. Get up, get out, and get something. Go get what God has for you! Be empowered.

Life Tools:

2 Corinthians 12:9 NIV "But he said to me, "My grace is sufficient for you, for my power is made perfect in weakness." Therefore I will boast all the more gladly about my weaknesses, so that Christ's power may rest on me."

Deuteronomy 31:6 NLT "So be strong and courageous! Do not be afraid and do not panic before them. For the LORD your God will personally go ahead of you. He will neither fail you nor abandon you."

CHOOSE TO SHOW MERCY

Compassionate treatment toward someone who you really could be mean and nasty to is what it means to show mercy. How many times do you get angry with people and fly off the deep end? They made me mad, so I am going to give them a piece of my mind. They better not ever ask me for anything again. Next time they do this, I'm going to tell them off. Yup, been there done that. My point is this, no one is perfect. You make mistakes, I make mistakes, we all do. That's just a part of life and you expect people to have mercy on you. You expect people to forgive you when you wrong them, sometimes whether you ask for that forgiveness or not. Yet, find it virtually impossible to show that same mercy towards someone else. Why is that? To me, this goes back to the simple principle of the golden rule. Aren't you supposed to treat people the same way you want to be treated?

Taking this a little bit deeper, God shows you mercy each and every day. He knows that you have fallen short of His Glory. He continues to love on you, bless you, protect you, and provide for you in spite of your shortcomings. He does so because He is just that kind of God. When I think about mercy, I'm always reminded of John 8, where the lady is caught in adultery and the people are ready to stone her to death. Jesus steps in and tells them, "He without sin, let him throw the first stone". I love that story because as I said earlier is just seems like everyone is quick to point the finger at others and throw stones, when truth be told you should have a few bricks thrown right back at you. We hand folks over to God's mercy, yet show none ourselves and that is just not right.

Think about that the next time you are ready to call somebody out and start pointing fingers. We all have our faults. Your fault may be different than mine, but it does not make one any worse than the other. A sin is a sin, but God's love supersedes all. Do not beat yourself up over your mistakes and do not beat anyone else up over theirs. Instead choose to show mercy. This day and every day I want you to remember that you are clothed with God's tenderhearted mercy. How greatly God has blessed you! How greatly God truly loves you! Now turn around and show that same mercy to someone else.

Life Tools:

Psalms 86:5 KJV "For thou, Lord, art good, and ready to forgive; and plenteous in mercy unto all them that call upon thee."

Ephesians 2:4 ESV "But God, being rich in mercy, because of the great love with which he loved us"

Titus 3:5 NLT "He saved us, not because of the righteous things we had done, but because of his mercy. He washed away our sins, giving us a new birth and new life through the Holy Spirit."

THAT'S JUST WHO YOU ARE

I'm sure you've heard the saying, 'don't mistake my kindness for weakness'. You've probably even had to tell a few people those exact words a time or two. This is basically saying that just because I am nice, I will not be taken advantage of. Now, let's look at the flip side of this. Why are you nice? We were all taught the golden rule growing up; treat others how you want to be treated. So, are you nice because you want others to be nice to you? Are you nice because you are expecting something in return? Or are you nice because that is just who you are? The best obvious answer of course would be because that's just who you are. Ok, got it. So let me give you this scenario and see if this gets you thinking...

There's a person who you help out, give things too and consider to be a friend. You see them one day and they act as if they don't even know who you are. Not only do they not speak, but when you speak to them, they look you dead in the eye and completely ignore you. What is your initial response? Do you get mad because of how "kind" or "nice" you have been to them in the past? If the answer is yes, which let's just be honest, that's going to be most people's answer, then you have to go back to my initial question. Why are you nice? My point here is that you have to acknowledge that good or bad sometimes your behavior is motivated. Motivated by what, just depends on you. If your motives are truly right, then the behavior of other people won't determine whether you are nice or nasty. You will keep being you because that's just who you are. Kindness is a character trait. It is not something you can simply take off the shelf and put it on like an outfit when you want to. If you are doing that, then guess what, being kind is just not a part of who you really are.

Kindness is one of the most valuable gifts you will ever give someone. No act of kindness, no matter how small or insignificant you may think it is, is ever waster. So if someone I've been kind to stops speaking to me or act as though they don't know me, I have decided that I will take that as a lesson learned about them. I will not allow it to hinder me from being me and showing kindness towards people. Having experienced this first hand, I have to admit this is truly a tough pill to swallow. I know however, that with the help of God nothing is impossible. Even concerning your emotions and especially concerning your character.

The Bible says that we are the likeness of Christ. I believe wholeheartedly that in order to be so, there are certain things about you that you are just going to have to get together. This issue here is one of them. Do not like anyone so much that you allow them to pull you away from the likeness of Christ. Be thankful when you learn who people are for real, but I'll say it again, don't let that change who you are.

Life Tools:

Luke 6:35 ESV "But love your enemies, and do good, and lend, expecting nothing in return, and your reward will be great, and you will be sons of the Most High, for he is kind to the ungrateful and the evil."

Ephesians 4:32 NIV "Be kind and compassionate to one another, forgiving each other, just as in Christ God forgave you."

Proverbs 11:17 ESV "A man who is kind benefits himself, but a cruel man hurts himself."

WILL YOU INVITE HIM IN?

God is always trying to work in and through you. He's trying to work in your family, in your job, in your situations and in your circumstances. He is Immanuel, God with you. He is Jehovah Shammah, ever present. He calls himself I AM, not I was or I will be, which means He is present right now ready to work in your life. Now that I have enlightened you with this great piece of information, do you think this will change anything in your present life? If not, it should. It should give you a better perspective of just who God is. As your relationship with God grows, it is easier to understand the many facets of who He is. Before the relationship can grow, it must first be established. God is such a gentleman. He will not force Himself on anyone. He must be invited in. Once you give Him the invitation and welcome Him in, He begins to remold you and make you into what His original intention was before the craziness of this world got a hold to you.

For me personally, knowing that God is with me gives me confidence. I am able to walk in that peace that Paul talks about in Philippians 4:7. The peace of God that surpasses all understanding. It makes me feel as though no matter what is going on around me, good or bad, I am taken care of. No matter what tactics the enemy uses to try and attack, I am alright. Why? Because God is with me.

Have you invited Christ into your life as your personal Lord and Savior? I have invited Him into my life. I am absolutely nothing without God and neither are you. None of us are. I tell Him each and every day how much I need Him and I thank Him for loving me enough to never leave me. God is no respecter of persons. He does not show favoritism, so that means He loves you just as much as He loves me and everyone else in this world. Even when we sin, He still loves us. Even when we don't love ourselves, He loves us. I can truly testify that the remolding can sometimes be a tough process, but the end result will be pure excellence. Will you invite Him in?

Life Tools:

Romans 10:9-10 NIV "If you declare with your mouth, "Jesus is Lord," and believe in your heart that God raised him from the dead, you will be saved. For it is with your heart that you believe and are justified, and it is with your mouth that you profess your faith and are saved."

Psalms 46:1 KJV "God is our refuge and strength, a very present help in trouble."

Philippians 4:7 ESV "And the peace of God, which surpasses all understanding, will guard your hearts and your minds in Christ Jesus."

*****If you want to accept Jesus Christ as your Lord and Personal Savior right now, pray this prayer…*****

Heavenly Father, I come to you in the name of Jesus. I acknowledge that I am a sinner. I am sorry for my sins and I repent. Please God, forgive me. I need your forgiveness.

I believe that your only begotten Son, Jesus Christ shed His precious blood on the cross at Calvary and died for my sins, and I am now willing to turn from my sin.

You said in Your Holy Word, that if we confess the Lord our God and believe in our hearts that God raised Jesus from the dead, we shall be saved.

Right now I confess Jesus as the Lord of my soul. With my heart, I believe that God raised Jesus from the dead. This very moment I accept Jesus Christ as my own personal Savior and according to His Word, right now I am saved.

Thank you Jesus for your unlimited grace which has saved me from my sins. I thank you Jesus that your grace never leads to license, but rather it always leads to repentance. Therefore Lord Jesus transform my life so that I may bring glory and honor to you alone and not to myself.

Thank you Jesus for dying for me and giving me eternal life.

Amen.

***If you just said this prayer and you meant it with all your heart and you have repented for your sins, I believe that you just got saved and are born again. Congratulations on making the very best decision you could ever make in life.**

CONCLUSION

You'll notice the ending to just about every section in this book encouraged you to seek God, pray or study your word. Reason being is because God is the source, strength, motivator, encourager and the very reason why you are alive today. Jesus is your Lord and it is time you treated Him as such. He is your savior, but He should also be Lord over your life. Lord means the head. On a human the head is on top, so He should be over top of you. On an animal the head is in front, so He should be leading you. Make Jesus Lord of your life. Include Him in every aspect of your life. When you wake up in the morning, ask the Holy Spirit to guide and direct you in everything you do.

You are a product of what you have been speaking, believing and imagining. What words are coming out of your mouth? Say what you mean and mean what you say. That small tongue of yours is a very powerful tool. You need to use it wisely. What are you believing God for? Do you really believe that all things are possible with Christ Jesus? Are you able to imagine a life without limits? Look beyond your right now. There is greatness inside of you. It's time to reach down and pull it out.

In this life, you have to take the bitter with the sweet. God will send both your way because both will shape you into the person He created you to be. If I can step out on faith in what I felt to be a bitter time in my life and start writing this book, you can too. Your journey may not include writing, it may be singing. Whatever it is, no better time than now to get it done. When you do it, let excellence be the signature upon all you say and do. Show the devil that you might get knocked down, but you will never stay there. You will only get back up stronger, wiser and more determined to reach your destiny.

I wish I could say that I have it all figured out. I wish I could tell you that life will be easy. Instead I will say that the fight will not be easy. At times, the heartbreak will feel like physical pain in your body. The memories may even creep into your mind and make your heart cry. It is ok. You will be ok. If I can make it, so can you. Don't give up. Do not quit. Fight back and let your scars remind you that you walk among survivors, wounded for a purpose. As it says in 2 Timothy 3:12, everyone who wants to live a Godly life in Christ Jesus will be persecuted. If Jesus had to endure, you will too.

Whatever problem, trial, tribulation, or obstacle you may be going through right now I decree and declare over your life that you got this! Why? Because God Got You! My last challenge to you is to awaken every morning to live the life of your dreams. You can talk about life all day long, but now it is time for you to put some action behind those words. Ready, set, GO!

I speak this benediction upon your life
in Jesus name...
"May God Almighty bless you,
And make you fruitful and multiply you,
That you may be an assembly of peoples;
And give you the blessing of Abraham,
To you and your descendants with you,
That you may inherit the land

In which you are a stranger,
Which God gave to Abraham."
Genesis 28:3-4

Now unto Him who is able to do exceedingly
abundantly above all that we ask
or think, according to the power that works in us,
to Him be glory in the
church by Christ Jesus to all generations,
forever and ever. Amen.
Ephesians 3:20-21